CW00762832

Beauty in Letters

esolved Unanimously

THAT this Council desire t
on record and to express to
William W
al thanks for the valuable services
him during his tenure of the office of
MAYOR AND
MAGISTRATE
the outstanding ability and

JOHN P. WILSON

BEAUTY IN LETTERS

A SELECTION OF ILLUMINATED ADDRESSES

UNICORN

CONTENTS

FOREWORD

I wonder what art you find beautiful?

It is likely that you admire a variety of art, but have some particular favourites. I find illuminated manuscripts a joy. I am not thinking of medieval books of hours, admirable and interesting as they are; I am thinking more of the artwork from the Victorian times onwards when there emerged a fresh approach to calligraphy. Edward Johnston is thought to have rejuvenated a significant interest in lettering in the late nineteenth and early twentieth centuries, but the illuminated manuscripts to which I refer began earlier, in the early nineteenth century. These are the presentations and addresses to individuals in recognition of a long or distinguished service. I find these very beautiful, but also attractive for many other reasons.

They can have finely detailed calligraphy, embellished with small designs or pictures, requiring a commercial artist who is particularly skilled to produce fine art that is meant to be impressive. They can occur as folders, scrolls or certificates. The size and detail of the artwork, and the housing in which it is presented, would depend on how much the commissioner of the work was willing to spend. The more significant the recipient, the more impressive and expensive the presentation was liable to be. An Edwardian catalogue shows prices ranging from 2 guineas for a simple illumination in a plain folder to 25 guineas for a highly detailed embellished design in a gold frame. The decorative folder bindings, sometimes with metal engraved monograms, are additional, skilled and handsome works of art. What I find adds to their interest is that each one is unique, usually given to one person at a point in time as a celebration. They almost always represent a happy occasion. They provide a picture of a period in history and each will have a story behind why the presentation was made. They provide an opportunity to obtain an insight into someone's life and achievements, and allow a brief historical opening to social history.

You may wonder what it is about a picture that makes it an illumination. Usually 'illuminated' means the embellishment of lettering with gold, silver or colours.

The presentation of illuminations continues today, but on a very limited basis compared to the past. It is still possible to get the equivalent items by commissioning a calligrapher. The following can be of assistance:

SSI – The Society of Scribes & Illuminators https://calligraphyonline.org/commissions/

CLAS – The Calligraphy & Lettering Arts Society http://www.clas.co.uk/commissions/

The illuminated addresses presented within this book also illustrate a variety of lettering styles. Many of the Victorian examples use gothic lettering, a formal style established centuries ago. The style uses bold, decorative, upright letters and can be difficult to read. Even when later calligraphers employed lettering styles which are easier to read, such as italics, they might still have chosen to include some gothic letters. There are

Page 1 of the address to Alderman Sir James Ritchie, Bt given in 1902, illuminated by Sir J. Causten & Sons, London. *See p30 for more details.*

examples of illuminated addresses in this selection that include a variety of lettering styles within the same address. Illuminators are liable to have had freedom in the use of lettering and would have developed their own personal variations. Many illuminated addresses do not include the name of the illuminator, but where it is known the illuminator is named.

This book is created to share with you some of the beauty and artistic skills that exist within my accumulation of illuminated manuscripts. My interest started on a holiday to Scotland some years ago when I came across the illuminated addresses presented to the Earl of Hopetoun, when visiting Hopetoun House, near Edinburgh. I was struck by their beauty and artwork, and decided that I should try to acquire some.

The selection in this book covers a period of more than one hundred years, and the addresses have been given not only to individuals who may be wealthy or famous but also to ordinary people who have provided a special service. Some of the addresses were awarded before the individuals were honoured with titles. Where this has happened the name used is without the subsequent title. The examples selected are some of my favourites and cover a variety of topics. I trust that you will like them too.

There is one additional illuminated address included that is not in my collection. Rather, it belongs to the Bank of England, my employer, and is the only one to be found in its archives.

Thanks go to Erica Wilson for ornamental section break symbols, Chris Ison for most of the photography and Kathryn Willig for some vignettes.

This book is dedicated to my wife Rosemary who has tolerated me collecting items over the years and which now fill many bookshelves.

ARMED SERVICES

Soldier
Major John Walford

Captain John Walford was promoted to the rank of Major in 1882 and was presented with a stunning illuminated folder by his regiment. He was a major in the 1st Warwickshire Rifle Volunteer Corps No. 5 Company.

The Volunteer Corps was formed in 1859 as a result of a fear of a French invasion. In 1858 an Italian, Felice Orsini, threw bombs at the carriage of Emperor Napoleon III and his wife Eugénie in Paris. They were unharmed but eight others died and more than 140 were wounded. Orsini had obtained his explosives in England. The French public was outraged by the attack, believed there to be a British conspiracy and called for war. England was largely undefended due to Crimean commitments and so there was a call for a nationwide volunteer army. Emperor Napoleon III did not launch an attack, as he had other distractions, including, in 1859, a war with Austria.

There were many Warwickshire volunteer companies created. In due course these would see action in the Second Boer War and, after becoming part of the Territorial Force in 1908, the First and Second World Wars.

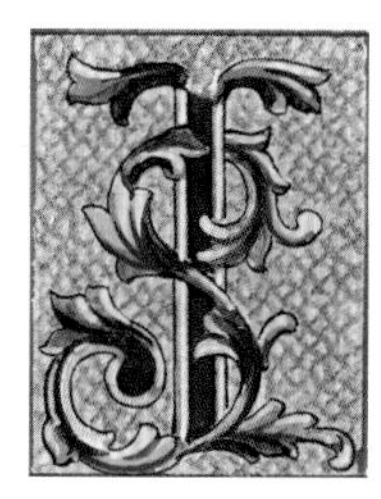

The address to Major John Walford given in 1882.

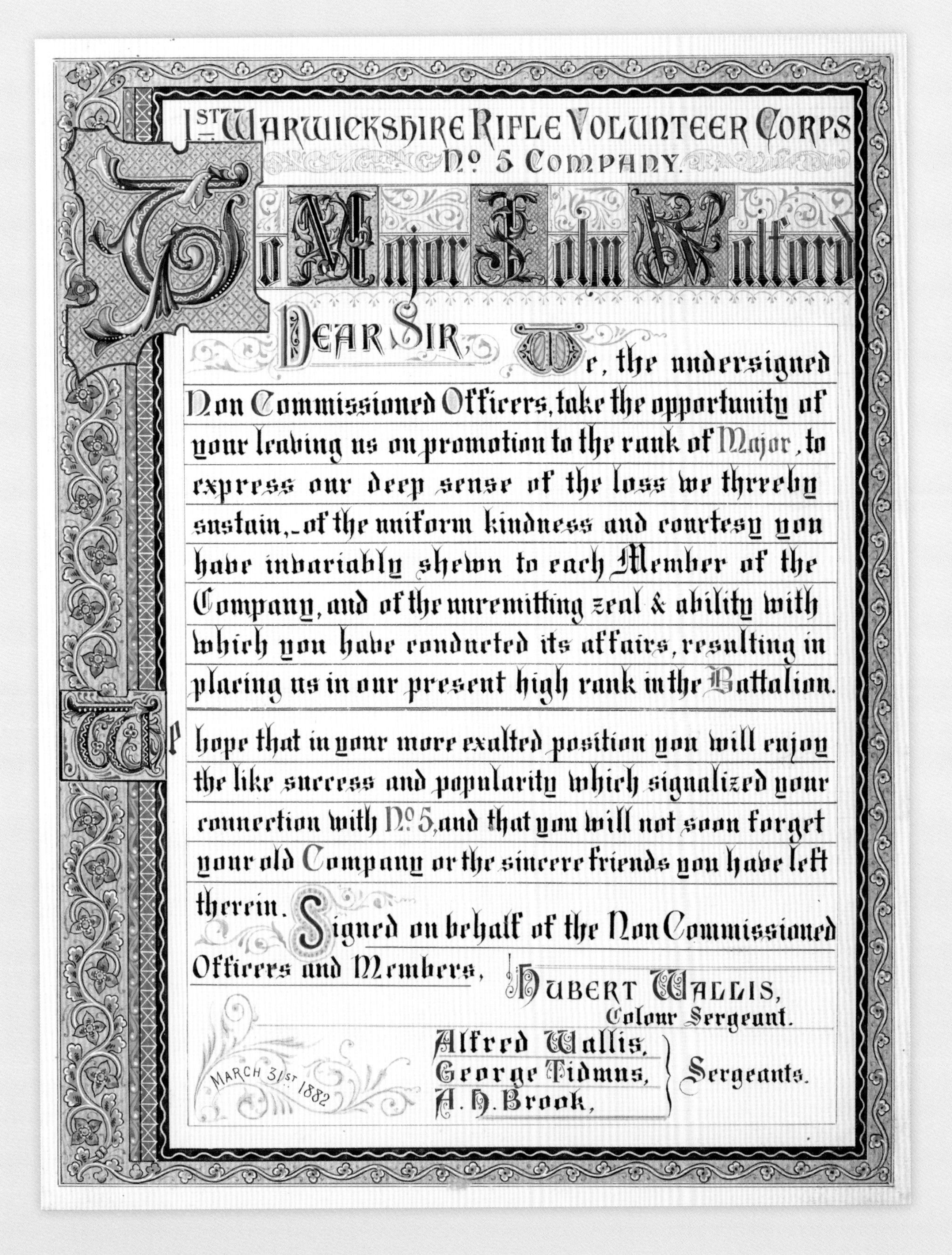

1st Warwickshire Rifle Volunteer Corps
No. 5 Company.

To Major John Walford

Dear Sir, We, the undersigned Non Commissioned Officers, take the opportunity of your leaving us on promotion to the rank of Major, to express our deep sense of the loss we thereby sustain, – of the uniform kindness and courtesy you have invariably shewn to each Member of the Company, and of the unremitting zeal & ability with which you have conducted its affairs, resulting in placing us in our present high rank in the Battalion.

We hope that in your more exalted position you will enjoy the like success and popularity which signalized your connection with No. 5, and that you will not soon forget your old Company or the sincere friends you have left therein. Signed on behalf of the Non Commissioned Officers and Members,

Hubert Wallis,
Colour Sergeant.

Alfred Wallis,
George Tidmus,
A. H. Brook,
Sergeants.

March 31st 1882

BUSINESS

HM Inspector of Taxes
Arthur G. Mead

Illuminated addresses were presented to a wide variety of people, including, on this occasion, an inspector of taxes.

Arthur Mead worked in Runcorn, Chester & District tax district and was given his gift on leaving to take up a position in London – presumably for a bigger, better job, perhaps in HM Treasury. Such a gift feels very generous, as he was only there for three years between 1922 and 1925.

The words in the address seem to stress the onerous nature of the work and the skills of tact and diplomacy shown by Mead. Unusually, this is endorsed by an additional statement at the end of the folder from the Special Commissioner of Taxes who repeats the earlier sentiments. He talks of the many 'delicate and difficult cases that have been so plentiful in this area during the trying times'.

The formal address of two pages is followed by five pages of eighty-four signatures. However, the majority of these are not Mead's colleagues in the tax office but rather local dignitaries and businesses. Individuals include the Superintendent of Police and three local clergymen. Forty-three local businesses are represented, often signed by the relevant managing director.

For those living near Runcorn today, the variety of signatures provides an interesting picture of the local businesses operating in 1922. Most of them probably would not be recognised, as they will have closed or been amalgamated into other businesses with a change of name. For instance, Greenall Whitley & Co. Ltd was probably a well-known brewery, as it had been running since its founding in 1762 in

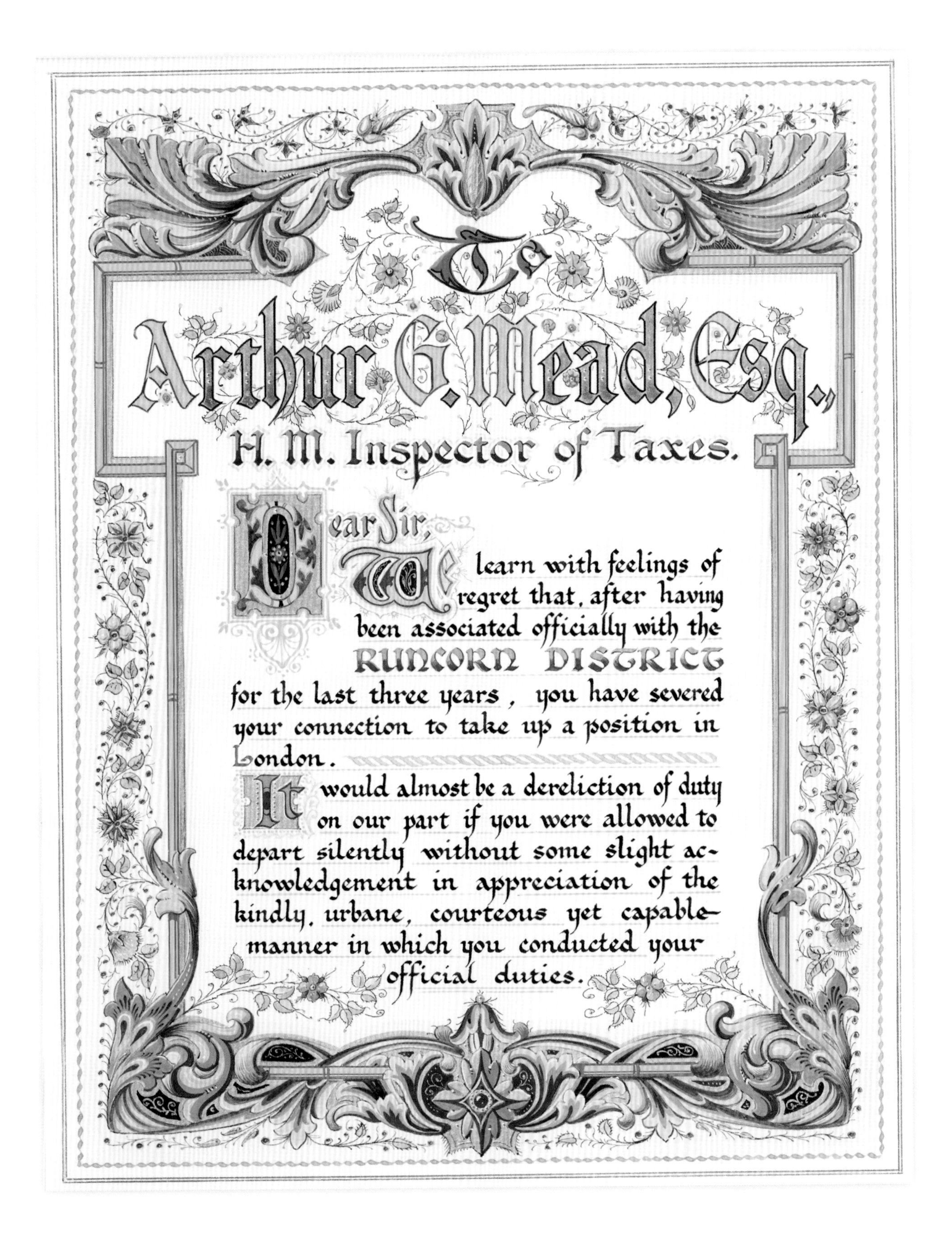
To
Arthur G. Mead, Esq.,
H. M. Inspector of Taxes.

Dear Sir,
We learn with feelings of regret that, after having been associated officially with the
RUNCORN DISTRICT
for the last three years, you have severed your connection to take up a position in London.
It would almost be a dereliction of duty on our part if you were allowed to depart silently without some slight acknowledgement in appreciation of the kindly, urbane, courteous yet capable manner in which you conducted your official duties.

It is for this reason that we wish to place on record the widespread feelings of esteem with which you are regarded by all sections of the community with whom you were officially brought in contact – from the smallest tax-payer to the largest.

Your duties, naturally of an onerous and conflicting character, were invariably done in such a painstaking, tactful manner as to leave no doubt of the sincerity of your intentions to mete out – even to the humblest tax-payer – absolute justice, and to inspire us with a belief in the genuine desire of the Department you represented to act fairly and uprightly – to hold the balance true between the Man and the State, without harshness on the one hand or favour on the other. In short you evoked and won the confidence of the Tax-payer and gave Citizenship an enhanced value of the Honour, the Dignity and the Integrity of the Inland Revenue Department.

Your unfailing kindliness and courtesy to all and sundry in the execution of your duties will long be remembered in the Runcorn area.

We wish you every success in your new sphere of action; and we appreciate to the full the new spirit of kindliness which now seeks to animate the great Department of State of which you are so able, so just, so painstaking an exponent.

Warrington, but it appears to have closed its last brewery in 1990. It is nice to see the signatures of the proprietors of businesses such as A. Timmins, General Manager of E. Timmins & Sons Ltd (Ebenezer Timmins of Bridgewater Foundry, Runcorn, iron founders and well-borers) and H.W. Handley of Horace W. Handley Ltd, iron mongers of 65 High Street, Runcorn.

The address to Arthur G. Mead given in 1925.

Insurance manager
Ernest Linnell

When Ernest Linnell retired in 1927, aged sixty-five, as General Manager of Sun Life Assurance Society, the directors agreed an annual pension for him of £5,000. Further, they awarded a gratuity of £10,000 for his exceptional value and service over a period of forty-four years, of which thirty-four were spent as Principal Officer. While he was in charge, the Society's funds increased from £3m to £30m.

Linnell also received a large and impressive illuminated address from the members of staff. The address provides the facts and figures for the Society since he had joined it in 1884, and would have been a helpful reminder of all the roles and names of the 106 staff in 1894 and the 634 staff in 1927.

Sun Life Assurance Society was a long-established and successful insurance company. It was established in 1810 with Joshua Milne as its first employee and appointed actuary. He published *A Treatise on the Valuation of Annuities and Assurances* in 1815, based on his studies to create new mortality tables using the mortality bills (burial statistics) of Carlisle. His work was subsequently used by many other life assurance companies.

Sun Life Assurance Society expanded by acquiring many similar companies. It was taken over in the 1990s first by UAP, a French insurer, and subsequently by AXA, which then sold part of its life assurance business to the Resolution Group, and later the other part to Phoenix Group.

Linnell was born on a farm in Northamptonshire in 1862. His father farmed 460 acres at Pury Hill in Plum Park and employed eight workers. The family was well-off, employing five servants. Linnell moved to Newington, London and was employed initially as an

Page 1 of the address to Ernest Linnell given in 1927 illuminated by Waterlow & Sons Ltd, London Wall.

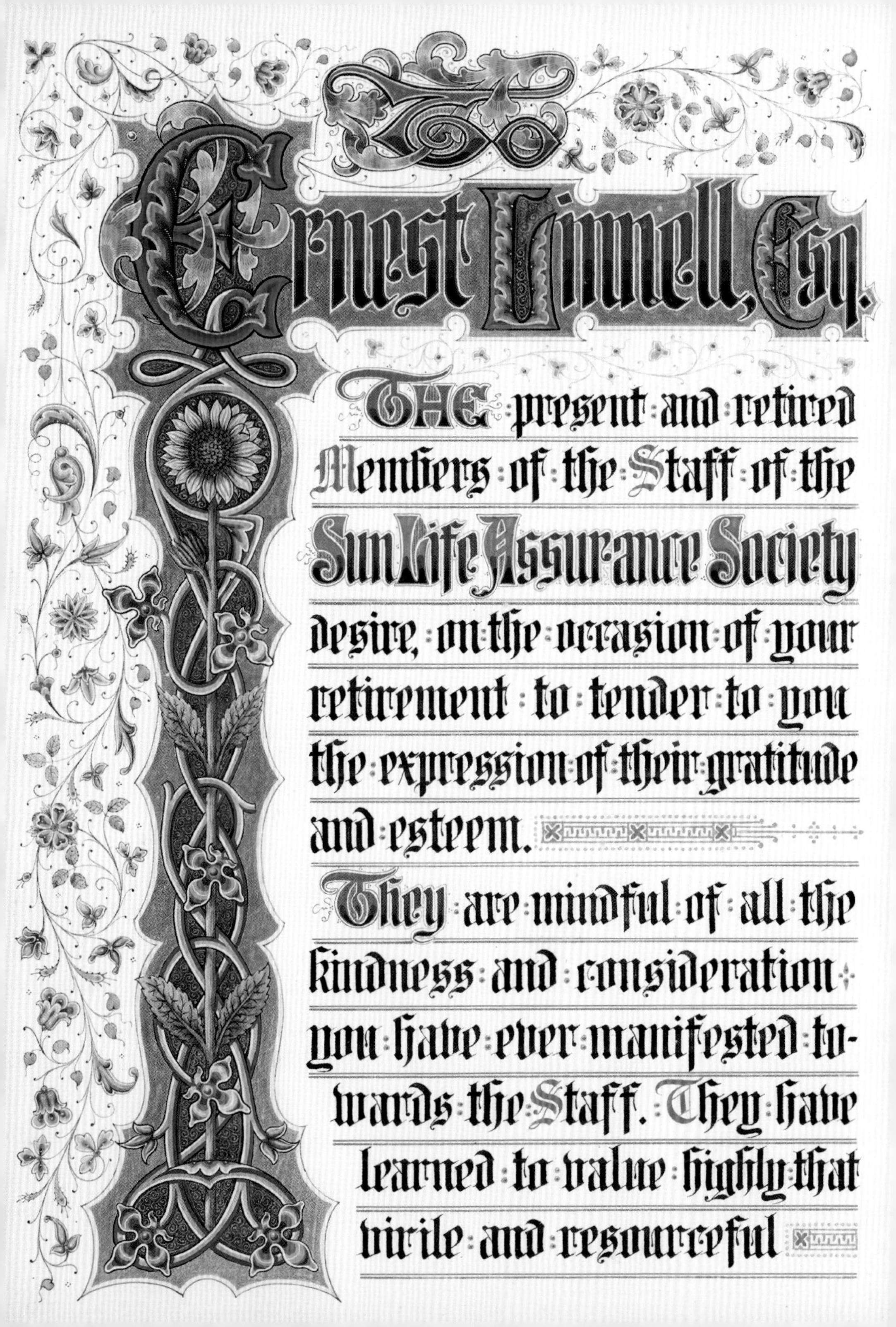

To
Ernest Linnell, Esq.

The present and retired Members of the Staff of the Sun Life Assurance Society desire, on the occasion of your retirement to tender to you the expression of their gratitude and esteem.

They are mindful of all the kindness and consideration you have ever manifested towards the Staff. They have learned to value highly that virile and resourceful

The address to Henry Adams given in 1905
illuminated by John Brown, 8 Gordon Street, Glasgow.

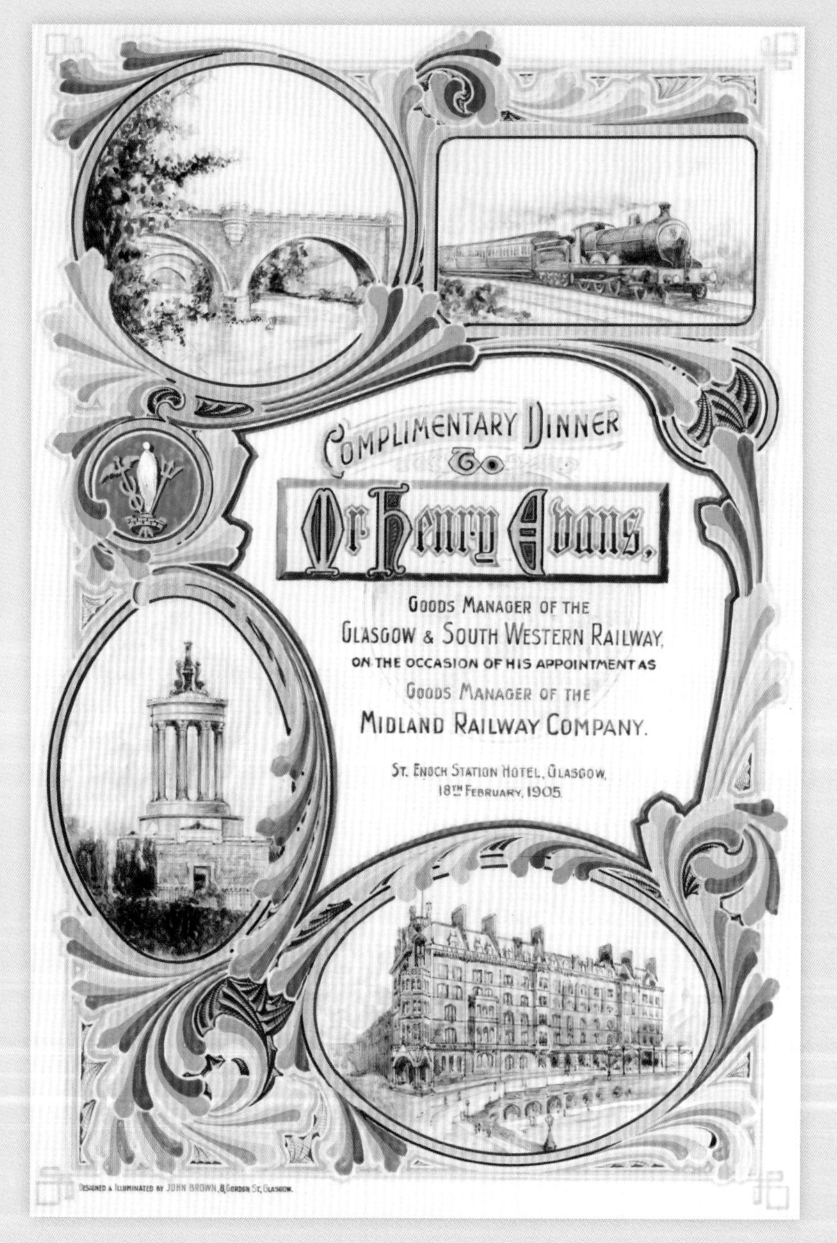

COMPLIMENTARY DINNER
TO
MR. HENRY EVANS,
GOODS MANAGER OF THE
GLASGOW & SOUTH WESTERN RAILWAY,
ON THE OCCASION OF HIS APPOINTMENT AS
GOODS MANAGER OF THE
MIDLAND RAILWAY COMPANY.

ST. ENOCH STATION HOTEL, GLASGOW,
18TH FEBRUARY, 1905.

DESIGNED & ILLUMINATED BY JOHN BROWN, 8 GORDON ST, GLASGOW.

CHAIRMAN
Sir John Ure Primrose Bart.
Lord Provost of the City of Glasgow.
CROUPIERS
Sir William Arrol, L.L.D. M.P.
Ex Deacon Convener Macfarlane, J.P.
Robert Angus Esq. J.P.
COMMITTEE
Sir William Arrol, L.L.D. M.P.
Ex Deacon Convener Mason D.L. J.P.
Ex Deacon Convener Macfarlane, J.P.
Robert Angus Esq. J.P.
George Ferguson Esq.

John Macfarlane.
Hon. Secy.

Mr. Henry Evans.

We, assembled in your honour, desire to offer you our hearty congratulations on your appointment as Goods Manager of the Midland Railway Company & to express the earnest hope that your success, so well merited in the past, will continue to attend you in years to come. We sincerely wish you, Mrs Evans and your family, length of days, good health, and all future happiness.

Railwayman
Henry Adams

In 1905 a dinner was held at the St Enoch Station Road Hotel in Glasgow to honour Henry Adams on his appointment as Goods Manager of the Midland Railway Company. Adams had previously been the Goods Manager of the Glasgow and South Western Railway.

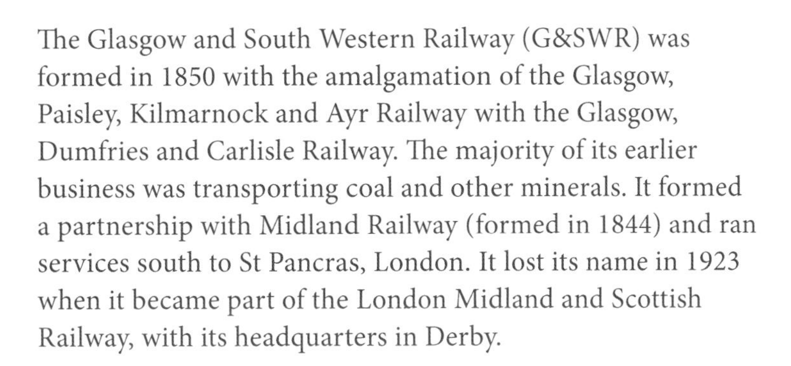

The Glasgow and South Western Railway (G&SWR) was formed in 1850 with the amalgamation of the Glasgow, Paisley, Kilmarnock and Ayr Railway with the Glasgow, Dumfries and Carlisle Railway. The majority of its earlier business was transporting coal and other minerals. It formed a partnership with Midland Railway (formed in 1844) and ran services south to St Pancras, London. It lost its name in 1923 when it became part of the London Midland and Scottish Railway, with its headquarters in Derby.

St Enoch Station Hotel was the headquarters of the G&SWR. The corresponding station no longer exists, as both the hotel and it were demolished in 1977.

Food manufacturer
Oliver Horlick

Oliver Horlick was aged seventy when, in 1955, he celebrated fifty years with the company Horlicks Limited, where he was the Chairman. He was presented with a thick volume which begins with an address.

Horlicks was an international company and it appears that every member of staff – home and abroad – signed the volume of ninety pages, many of those with twenty or more signatures. The overseas premises included Malaya, Ceylon, India and Belgium.

Examples of Liebig cards.

Horlicks is famous for its bedtime drink produced in its factory in Slough, Berkshire. However, it started as a baby food manufacturer. The business was created by brothers James and William Horlick, born in 1844 and 1846, respectively, in Gloucestershire. They began their working life as saddlers. William left for Wisconsin, USA to join a relative's building business and did well due to the extensive rebuilding needed after the1871 Great Chicago Fire. James became a chemist with the American Mellin Food Company which produced dried infant food based on a mix of malt and bran combined with milk and water (adapted from a mix known as Liebig's Extract) as a substitute for mother's milk. The formula was

adapted from the one created by the German chemist Justus von Liebig at the University of Giessen.

Liebig was interested in agriculture and how plants get their nutrients, and his work led to the development of the fertiliser industry. He also created a way of extracting products from beef, and these products were commercially developed by the Liebig Extract of Meat Company. The Liebig Company was based in Fray Bentos in Uruguay, where meat was cheap. It also created and developed the Oxo cube. The Liebig Company marketed itself in various ways, including developing cookery books, calendars and issuing more than 1,800 trade card sets.

Mellin sponsored the making of the UK's first airship in 1902, on which it used its advertising.

James Horlick decided to experiment with his own recipes. However, because he could not raise capital in London, in 1873 he decided to join his brother in the United States. The brothers formed J and W Horlick of Chicago and created a baby food business. They bought a farm with malting equipment and found their products popular. The brothers mixed malted barley and wheat flour with milk and evaporated it until it became a fine powder. The powder could later be added to fresh milk and water to create an attractive drink.

James returned to London to create the Horlicks Malted Milk Company in 1906, with a factory in Ploughlees Farm, near Slough. Like the Liebig Extract of Meat Company and the Mellin Food Company, Horlicks Malted Milk Company used advertising widely. The drink became popular in England and gained fame by providing supplies to Ernest Shackleton's Antarctic expeditions. James was created a Baron in 1914 and died in 1921. William died aged ninety in 1936. Their four sons inherited the business.

The business was sold to SmithKline Beecham for £20m in 1969.

The address to Oliver Horlick given in 1955 illuminated by 'SHEP'.

LABORE
ET
SCIENTIA
RACINE. WIS:
NOWRA.N.S.W
PRESENTED TO
OLIVER
HORLICK ESQ
ON THE OCCASION OF HIS
SEVENTIETH BIRTHDAY
AND THE COMPLETION OF
HIS FIFTIETH YEAR OF
SERVICE WITH THE COMPANY.
FROM HIS FELLOW DIRECTORS
AND THE STAFFS OF THE
HORLICKS GROUP OF COMPANIES
AT HOME AND OVERSEAS AS
A VERY SINCERE TOKEN OF
THEIR GOOD WISHES
AND ESTEEM
ILMINSTER
TAUNTON
NEWTON ABBOT
MINEHEAD
SLOUGH
BUCKS
SHEP

Mill owner
Sir W. Henry (Harry) Hornby, Bt, MP

Here are two illuminations in very different styles.

The first impressive illuminated address, with an equally elaborate tooled cover with a central coat of arms, is housed in a box with a metal monogram.

It was given to Sir Harry by the workers at his cotton-spinning and weaving factory, founded in 1828, at Brookhouse Mill, Blackburn in 1899 when he received his baronetcy. The presentation recognises Sir Harry's contributions as mayor, MP and Chairman of the Education Committee. However, just as importantly it appreciates Sir Harry's concern, support for and kindness to his employees.

Cover of the address to Sir W. Henry Hornby, Bt, MP given in 1899, illuminated by Dugdale & Sons, Blackburn.

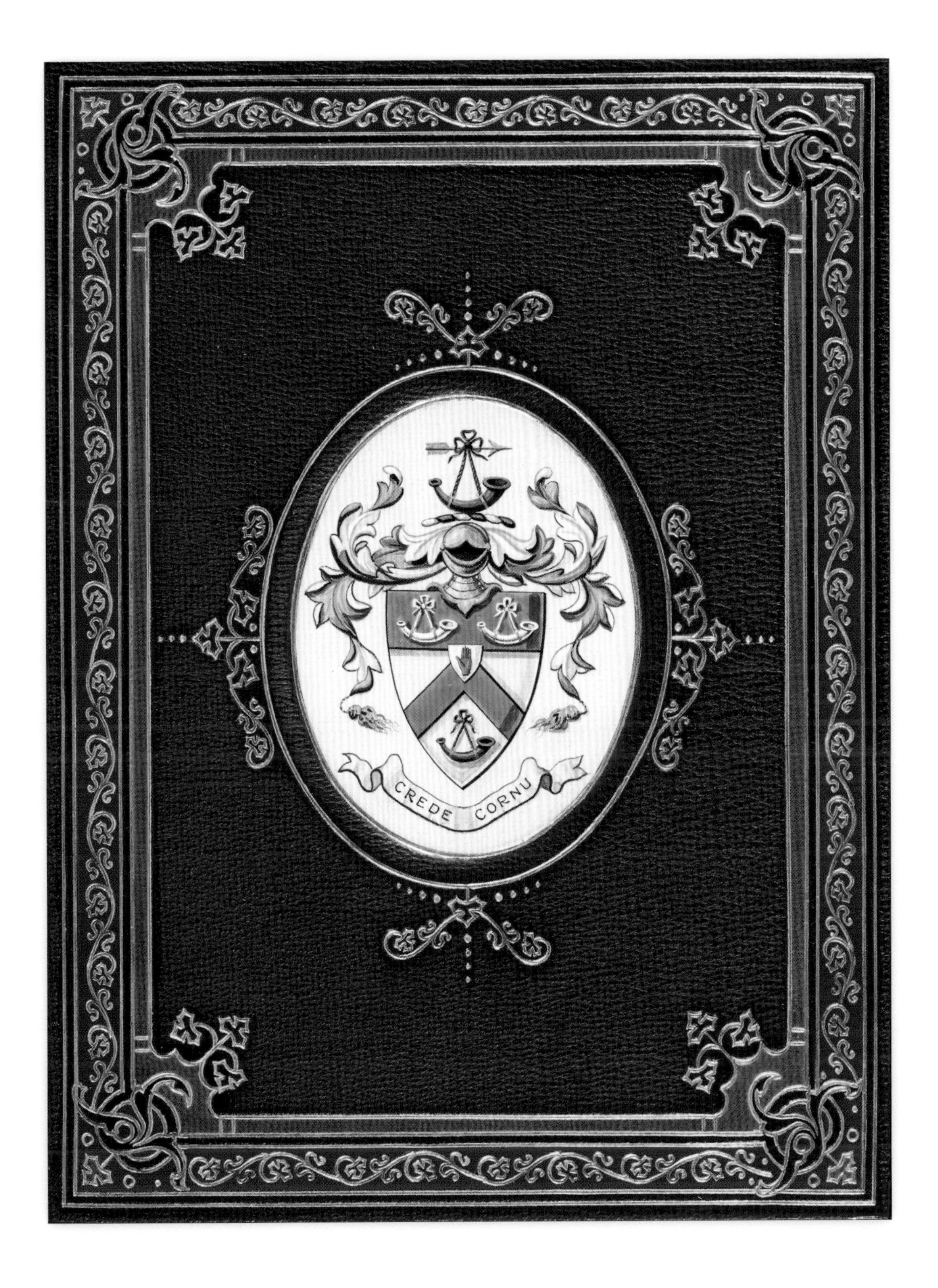
CREDE CORNU

ARTE ET LABORE

To

Sir Harry Hornby

Baronet, M.P.

Dear Sir,

We, the undersigned, representing the great body of our fellow-workers employed at your Brookhouse Mills, Blackburn, are most desirous of spontaneously offering you our Sincere Congratulations on your receiving, from Her Gracious Majesty the Queen, the high honour of a Baronetcy in the New Years' List of the Year of Grace 1899. We cannot but realise, with the great body of our and your fellow-townsmen, that so great an honour

Dugdale & Son, Illuminators, Blackburn.

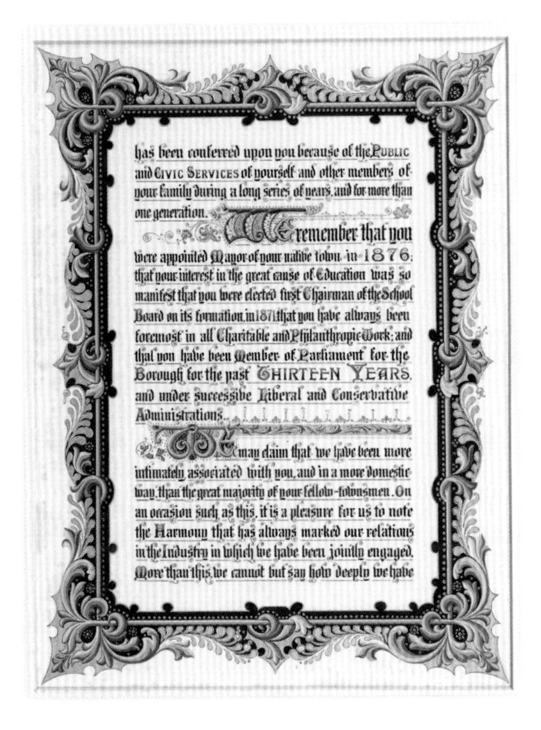

has been conferred upon you because of the Public and Civic Services of yourself and other members of your family during a long series of years, and for more than one generation.

We remember that you were appointed Mayor of your native town in 1876; that your interest in the great cause of Education was so manifest that you were elected first Chairman of the School Board on its formation in 1871; that you have always been foremost in all Charitable and Philanthropic Work; and that you have been Member of Parliament for the Borough for the past THIRTEEN YEARS, and under successive Liberal and Conservative Administrations.

We may claim that we have been more intimately associated with you, and in a more domestic way, than the great majority of your fellow-townsmen. On an occasion such as this, it is a pleasure for us to note the Harmony that has always marked our relations in the Industry in which we have been jointly engaged. More than this, we cannot but say how deeply we have

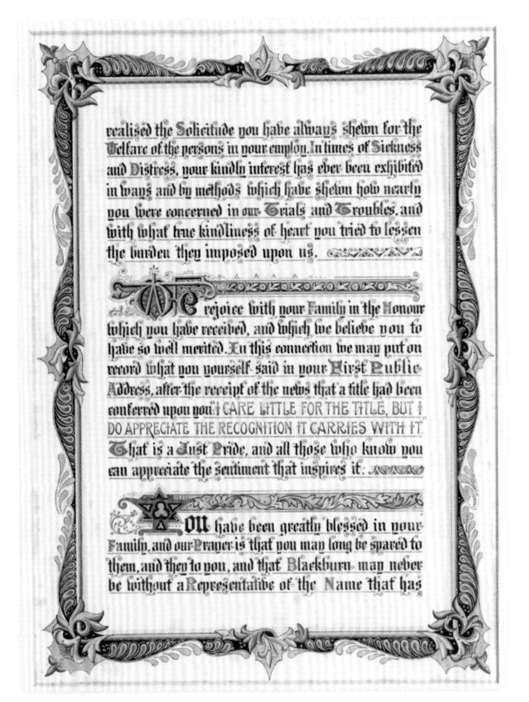

realised the Solicitude you have always shewn for the Welfare of the persons in your employ. In times of Sickness and Distress, your kindly interest has ever been exhibited in ways and by methods which have shewn how nearly you were concerned in our Trials and Troubles, and with what true kindliness of heart you tried to lessen the burden they imposed upon us.

We rejoice with your Family in the Honour which you have received, and which we believe you to have so well merited. In this connection we may put on record what you yourself said in your First Public Address, after the receipt of the news that a title had been conferred upon you: "I CARE LITTLE FOR THE TITLE, BUT I DO APPRECIATE THE RECOGNITION IT CARRIES WITH IT." That is a Just Pride, and all those who know you can appreciate the sentiment that inspires it.

You have been greatly blessed in your Family, and our Prayer is that you may long be spared to them, and they to you, and that Blackburn may never be without a Representative of the Name that has

Pages 2, 3 and 4 of the address to Sir W. Henry Hornby, Bt, MP given in 1899.

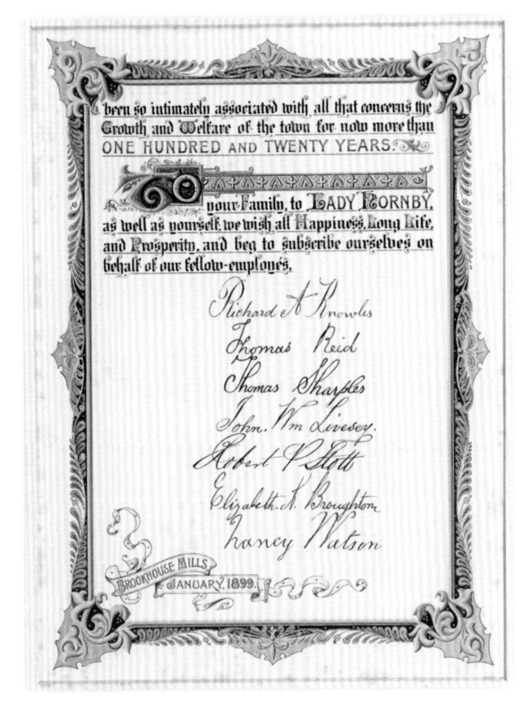

been so intimately associated with all that concerns the Growth and Welfare of the town for now more than ONE HUNDRED AND TWENTY YEARS.

To your Family, to LADY HORNBY, as well as yourself, we wish all Happiness, Long Life, and Prosperity, and beg to subscribe ourselves on behalf of our fellow-employés,

Richard A. Knowles
Thomas Reid
Thomas Sharples
John Wm Livesey.
Robert V. Stott
Elizabeth A. Broughton
Nancy Watson

BROOKHOUSE MILLS
JANUARY, 1899.

Page 1 of the address to Sir W. Henry Hornby, Bt, MP given in 1899, illuminated by Dugdale & Sons, Blackburn.

The second illuminated address, also of 1899, is much simpler. It is in the format of an embellished letter with gentle watercolour pictures, presented in an encased frame. This was in gratitude to his opening of St Anne's New School.

Sir Harry's younger brother Albert Neilson Hornby was probably better known to the public as he was a cricketer, rugby player and football player. He was selected for Test matches in 1878 and 1882 against Australia. The 1882 match was lost by England and gave rise to the Ashes, when the *Sporting Times* reported that English cricket has died '… the body will be cremated and the ashes taken to Australia'. A.N. Hornby played for England in the first 15-a-side Rugby International against Ireland in 1877 and captained England in 1882 in a win against Scotland. He also played football for Blackburn Rovers in their inaugural game in 1878.

The second illuminated address to Sir W. Henry Hornby, Bt, MP given in 1899.

Sir W. H. Hornby Bart. M.P.

Dear Sir,

Most heartily do we welcome you to our New Schools and we thank you very sincerely for coming to open the Sale of Work, a kindness which we appreciate highly as we fully realise the many calls upon your valuable time.

You have always taken a deep interest in the welfare of your townspeople and all Blackburn rejoiced in the honour but recently conferred upon you, its Senior Representative. We too, the children of St. Anne's Schools would offer you our congratulations, and we pray that God may long spare you and Lady Hornby to enjoy it, and health, happiness, and every blessing.

Thanking you again for opening our Sale of Work and New Schools,

We remain,

Yours respectfully,

The children of

St. Anne's.

April 27th 1899.

Chairman
Alderman Sir James Ritchie, Bt

Alderman Sir James Ritchie, Bt was Lord Mayor of London in 1903. He was also Chairman of the Jute Association for twenty-eight years and was presented in 1902 with one of my favourite and earliest illuminations, with every page full of exquisite designs.

There are many words from the past that are little used today. Although they may be recognisable, I find that I need a reminder of what they mean. One such word is 'jute', a plant and the name of the fibre from which it comes. It is between 3 ft and 13 ft in length, from which the fibres can be spun into long threads and then into hessian and other cloth. It is versatile and cheap, like cotton. In the 1600s the East India Company started trading in jute, a staple product of the area now known as Bangladesh. Jute was used by the military and British jute traders gained wealth.

Dundee was one centre for the jute business and the East India Company set up jute mills in Bengal, with many Scots emigrating to set up jute factories. More than a billion jute sandbags were used in the trenches in the First World War and they were also used in the United States to bag cotton. Jute was used in fishing, construction, art and the arms industries. Initially it could only be processed by hand until, in Dundee, it was found that if treated with whale oil it could be processed by machine. The industry boomed in the eighteenth and nineteenth centuries but declined in the twentieth century due to the alternative use of synthetic fibres.

Page 1 of the address to Alderman Sir James Ritchie, Bt given in 1902, illuminated by Sir J. Causten & Sons, London.

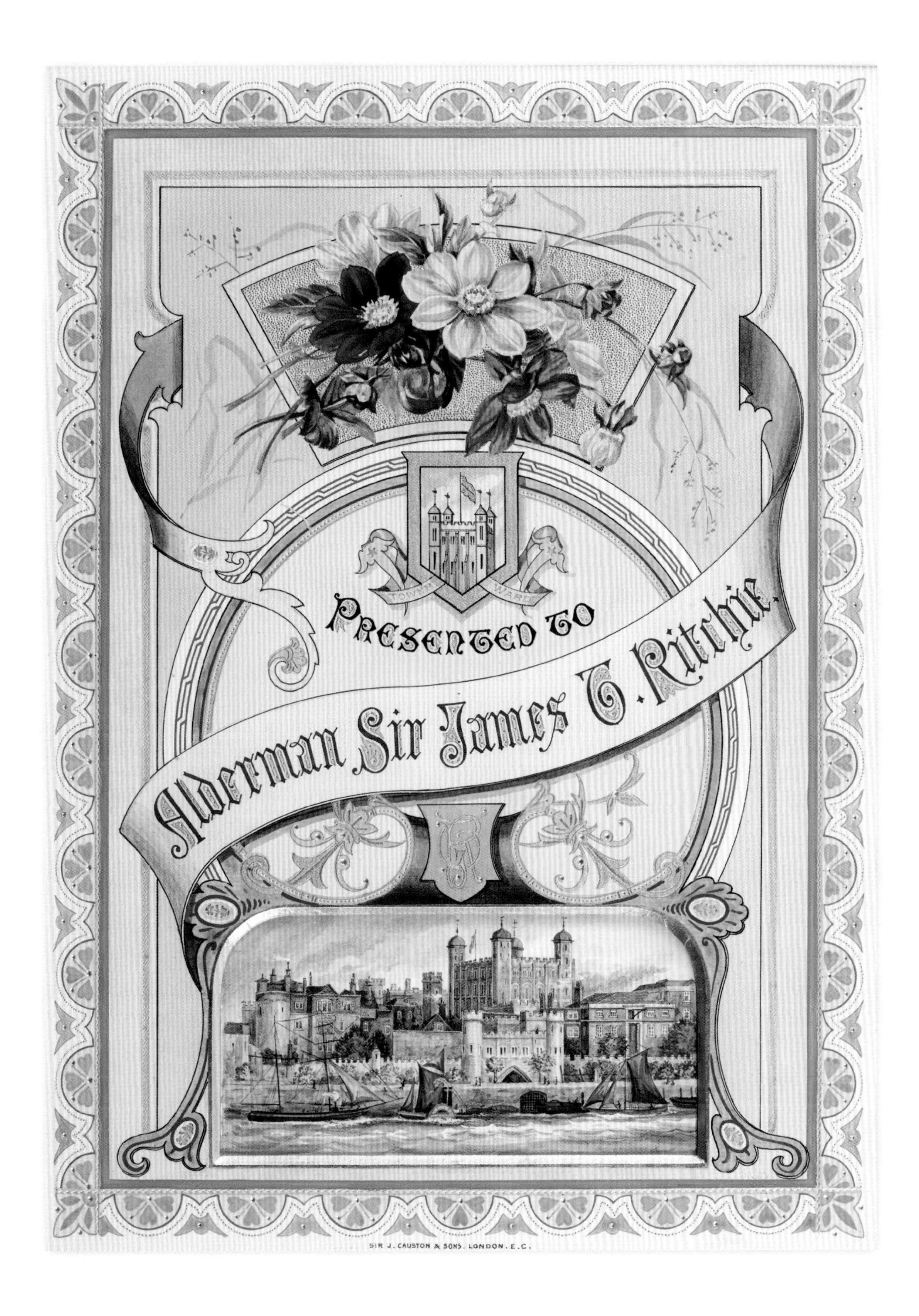
TOWER WARD
PRESENTED TO
Alderman Sir James T. Ritchie.
SIR J. CAUSTON & SONS. LONDON. E.C.

Alderman Sir James T. Ritchie.

Domine Dirige Nos

We the undersigned Members of the

London Jute Association

having been associated with you in the discharge of your duties, as first Chairman of the above association, which you have so successfully filled for the past 25 years, in asking your acceptance of a Silver Bowl, desire to express our grateful appreciation of your constant devotion to the interests of the association.

We congratulate you heartily that you have been enabled to fill this office for so long a period, during which time you have taken so active a part in the affairs of the Jute Trade in all its branches

Page 2 of the address.

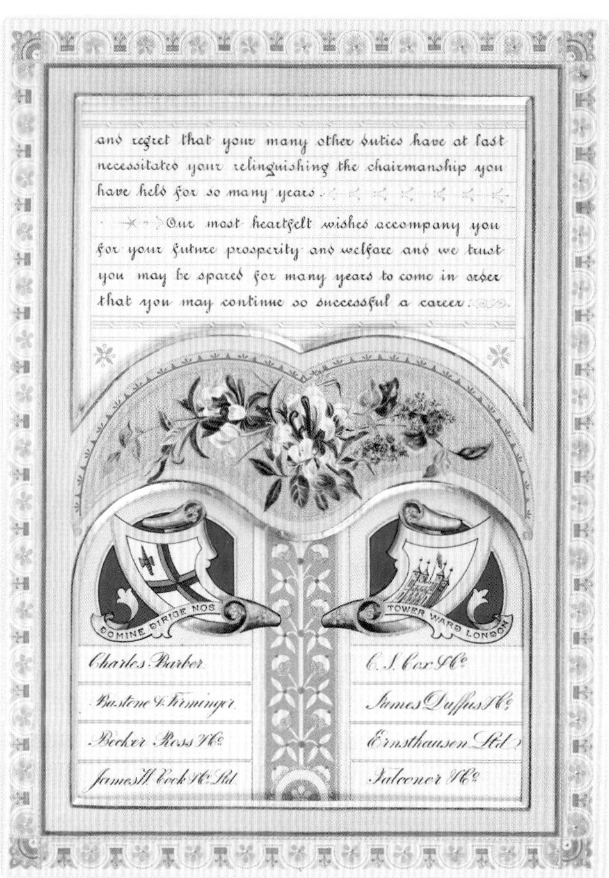

and regret that your many other duties have at last necessitated your relinquishing the chairmanship you have held for so many years.

Our most heartfelt wishes accompany you for your future prosperity and welfare and we trust you may be spared for many years to come in order that you may continue so successful a career.

Charles Barber. | C. S. Cox & Co.
Bastone & Firminger. | James Duffus & Co.
Becker Ross & Co. | Ernsthausen Ltd.
James W. Cook & Co. Ltd. | Falconer & Co.

Page 3 of the address.

Page 4 of the address.

One of the most successful jute-based businesses was run by the Ritchie family in Dundee. William Ritchie, father of Sir James, was head of the firm William Ritchie & Sons of London and Dundee.

Perhaps more famous than Sir James was his younger brother, Charles Ritchie, 1st Baron Ritchie of Dundee, who was Home Secretary from 1900–02 and Chancellor of the Exchequer from 1902–03 in Balfour's cabinet.

Another illuminated address to Sir James came to my collection separately a few years after the first. This was a single, framed picture. It was presented in 1904 by the workers at the Milners Safe Company Limited, operating at the Phoenix Safe Works in Liverpool to honour him for his appointment as Lord Mayor of London and gaining his baronetcy. Sir James was Chairman of the company.

Phoenix Safe Company still operates today. It describes itself as operating as the Richmond Safe Company Limited in 1799, supplying iron-clad wooden strong boxes and sea chests to the maritime trade. Steel reinforced strong boxes developed in Liverpool when a group of migrant workers from Toledo came to Liverpool en route to the United States. Instead, they joined the Richmond Safe Company, which was renamed the Withy Grove Stores in 1850 and the Phoenix Safe Company in 1986. The current company markets a wide range of security products.

The address to Sir James Ritchie, Bt, given in 1904, illuminated by W.A. Owens, Liverpool.

Phœnix Safe Works
Liverpool Sept 23rd 1904

To Sir James T. Ritchie Bart

Dear Sir James

We the Staff and Workpeople of Milners' Safe Company Limited desire respectfully to offer you our congratulations upon the success which has attended the Company's business during your able guidance as Chairman for the last 14 years & to take the opportunity of your presence here – for the purpose of laying the Memorial Stone of the Extension of the Works – to offer you this expression of our great esteem and our appreciation of the fairness and kindness which you have always shown us.

We are proud to see you occupying the High Office of Lord Mayor of the City of London & also at the honour conferred upon you by our beloved Sovereign King Edward VII.

We earnestly hope that you may long be spared to preside over us in carrying on the business of Milners' Safe Company Limited.

We are on behalf of the Staff and Workpeople
Your Obedient Servants.

W. H. Jones
SECRETARY

R. F. Whiteside
WORKS MANAGER

E. Kilner
CHIEF ACCOUNTANT

Arthur Fowler

Abel Hull
ASSISTANT WORKS MANAGER

Robert Taylor
SENIOR CORRESPONDENT

John Bright

William Lewis

William A. Owens
CHIEF DRAUGHTSMAN

H. J. Davies
SENIOR DEPOT MANAGER REPRESENTING DEPOTS

REPRESENTING THE WORKPEOPLE.

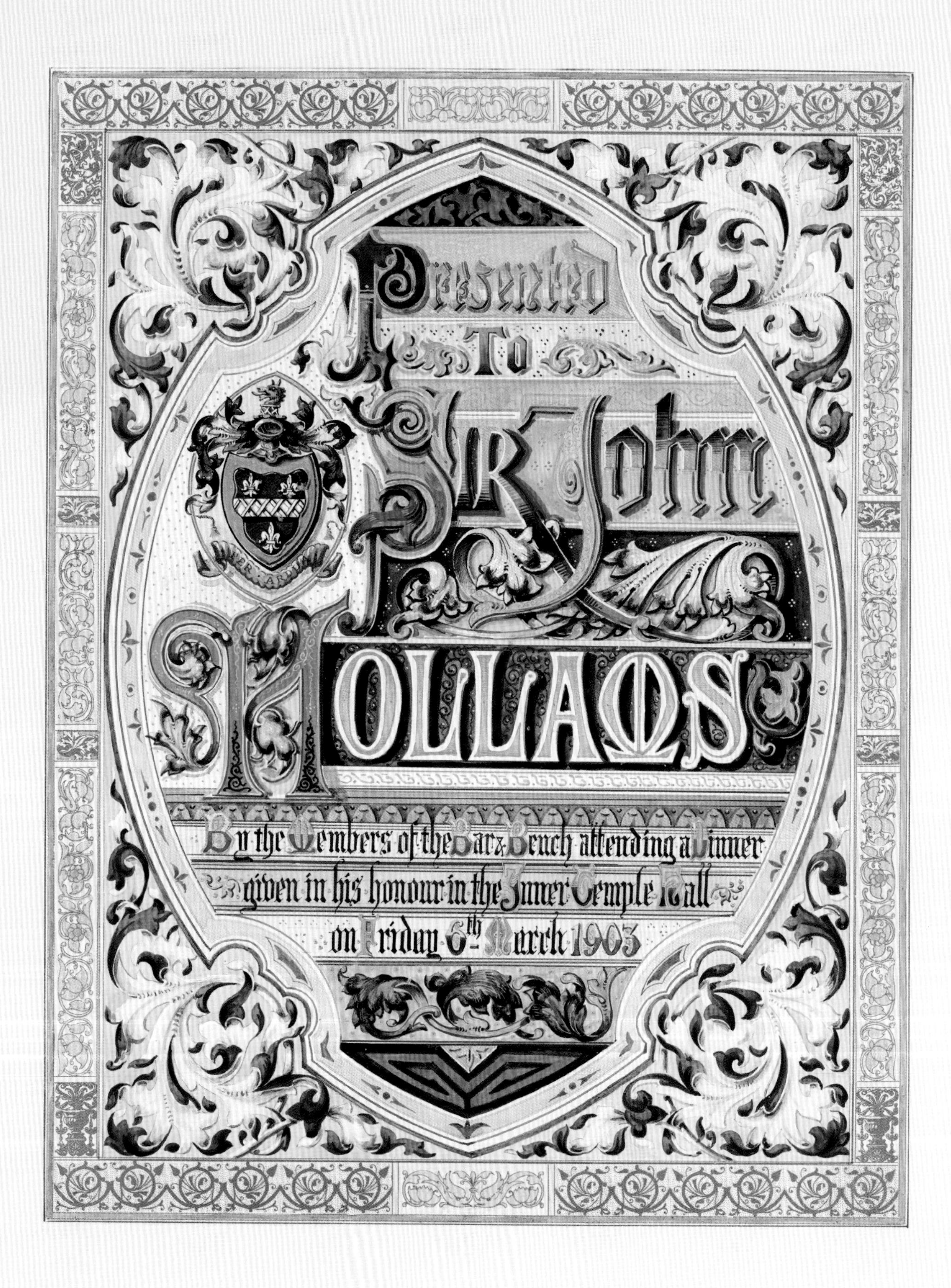
Presented
to
Sir John
Hollams
By the Members of the Bar & Bench attending a Dinner
given in his honour in the Inner Temple Hall
on Friday 6th March 1903
Per ardua

Lawyer
Sir John Hollams

In March 1903 a dinner was held at the Inner Temple Hall to honour Sir John Hollams and to celebrate his knighthood.

The dinner was a prestigious affair, with the most seniors members of the Bar and Bench present, paying their respects to Sir John following his long career in law. Afterwards, a large illuminated address was presented to Sir John by Lord James of Hereford. The address includes a table plan for the dinner and the signatures of all the guests. There were two toasts, one by the Lord Chancellor Lord Halsbury and the other by the Attorney General, Robert Finlay.

The top table included a number of noteworthy characters, including:

The Right Honourable Hardinge Giffard, 1st Earl of Halsbury, who during his life was appointed the Lord Chancellor three times, who was Grand Warden of the Freemasons and High Steward of the University of Oxford. He also complied the Halsbury's *Laws of England*, well-known to most lawyers.

Lord Alverstone, Lord Chief Justice, who was also President of the Surrey County Cricket Club.

Master of the Rolls, Richard Collins, later Baron Collins and Lord of Appeal in Ordinary.

Sir Roland Vaughan Williams, a Lord Justice of the Court of Appeal and uncle to the composer Ralph Vaughan Williams.

The address to Sir John Hollams given in 1903.

A page from the illuminated address

Sir James Stirling, a judge, and a Senior Wrangler at Cambridge. The Senior Wrangler is the student with the highest mathematics marks of those who achieve a first class degree in Mathematics at the university. He switched to law as he could not be admitted as a mathematics fellow because he was not a member of the Church of England.

Sir Edward Carson, a judge, who had earlier led the defence of the Marquess of Queensbury against the criminal libel action brought by Oscar Wilde. The Marquess used defamatory words about Oscar Wilde following the latter's relationship with his son, Lord Alfred Douglas. Wilde brought the action but abandoned his case before completion. He still had to pay costs,

The monogram on the front of the illuminated address cover.

including those of the defence, which he could not afford. He was taken to trial for gross indecency, found guilty and given a two year prison sentence.

Sir James Forrest Fulton, the Recorder of London. He was the judge who sat in the case of Adolf Beck, a famous Victorian fraud case. Beck was convicted of defrauding women of jewellery under a pseudonym, Lord Willoughby. He was convicted, but later given a pardon. A Committee of Inquiry was set up, led by the Master of the Rolls, Richard Collins, which found errors in the original trial evidence, and criticised Judge Fulton's conduct. The case led to the creation of the Court of Criminal Appeal.

The life story of Sir John Hollams is recorded in his autobiography *The Jottings as an Old Solicitor*, published by John Murray in 1906. Here he describes how the law changed during his working lifetime through the nineteenth century, from the time when he first came to London as a young man from his home in Loose, Kent, where his father had been the vicar.

Printer
Sir Philip Hickson Waterlow, Bt

Sir Philip Hickson Waterlow was a baronet, a Doctor of Letters and a Justice of the Peace.

You are likely to recognise the surname Waterlow as the name of the company famous for printing stamps, banknotes and share certificates. Waterlow as a business was founded in 1810. It lasted until 1961 when it was bought by Parnell & Sons. Soon after, Parnell & Sons sold it to De La Rue (the printers of Bank of England banknotes). Waterlow & Sons was started by James Waterlow in London, who created lithograph copies of legal documents. Lithography is a printing process using copies of a picture from an engraved plate.

Waterlow & Sons was involved in a famous trial related to the Portuguese Bank Note Crisis of 1925. The crisis was one of the biggest financial frauds in history with the Banco de Portugal as the victim. The fraud was created by Alves dos Reis, a Portuguese criminal, who drafted a contract for the Banco de Portugal to have Angolan banknotes printed.

The crisis unsettled the Portuguese economy, there was a coup d'état in 1926 and the government fell. It led to the dictatorship of Prime Minister António de Oliveira Salazar from 1932–68. The Banco de Portugal sued Waterlow & Sons in London, winning the case in 1932. Waterlow & Sons had to pay £610,000 in damages, and was never the same again. Sir William Waterlow, Bt, Sir Philip Waterlow, Bt's first cousin once removed, was dismissed as president of the company and died shortly afterwards.

Until 1928 HM Treasury issued treasury notes in England printed by Waterlow & Sons. After 1928 the Bank of England took control of bank

note issues and Waterlow & Sons lost the printing contract. De la Rue won the contract to print Bank of England banknotes from 2003.

James Waterlow, the founder of Waterlow & Sons, had five sons, four of whom joined the company. His fourth son, Sir Sydney Waterlow, became the 1st Baronet. Sir Sidney had five sons, the second of which was Sir Philip.

Sir Sydney was a philanthropist. He gave Waterlow Park in Highgate to the London County Council in 1889. Previously, he had given his home, Lauderdale House, in Waterlow Park to St Bartholomew's Hospital as a convalescent home for the poor. Nurses for the hospital were provided by Florence Nightingale. Lauderdale House dated from the sixteenth century and had been the home of the Duke of Lauderdale, and it is also thought to have been the home of Nell Gwyn, who King Charles II visited.

An engraving of Sir Philip Waterlow, Bt.

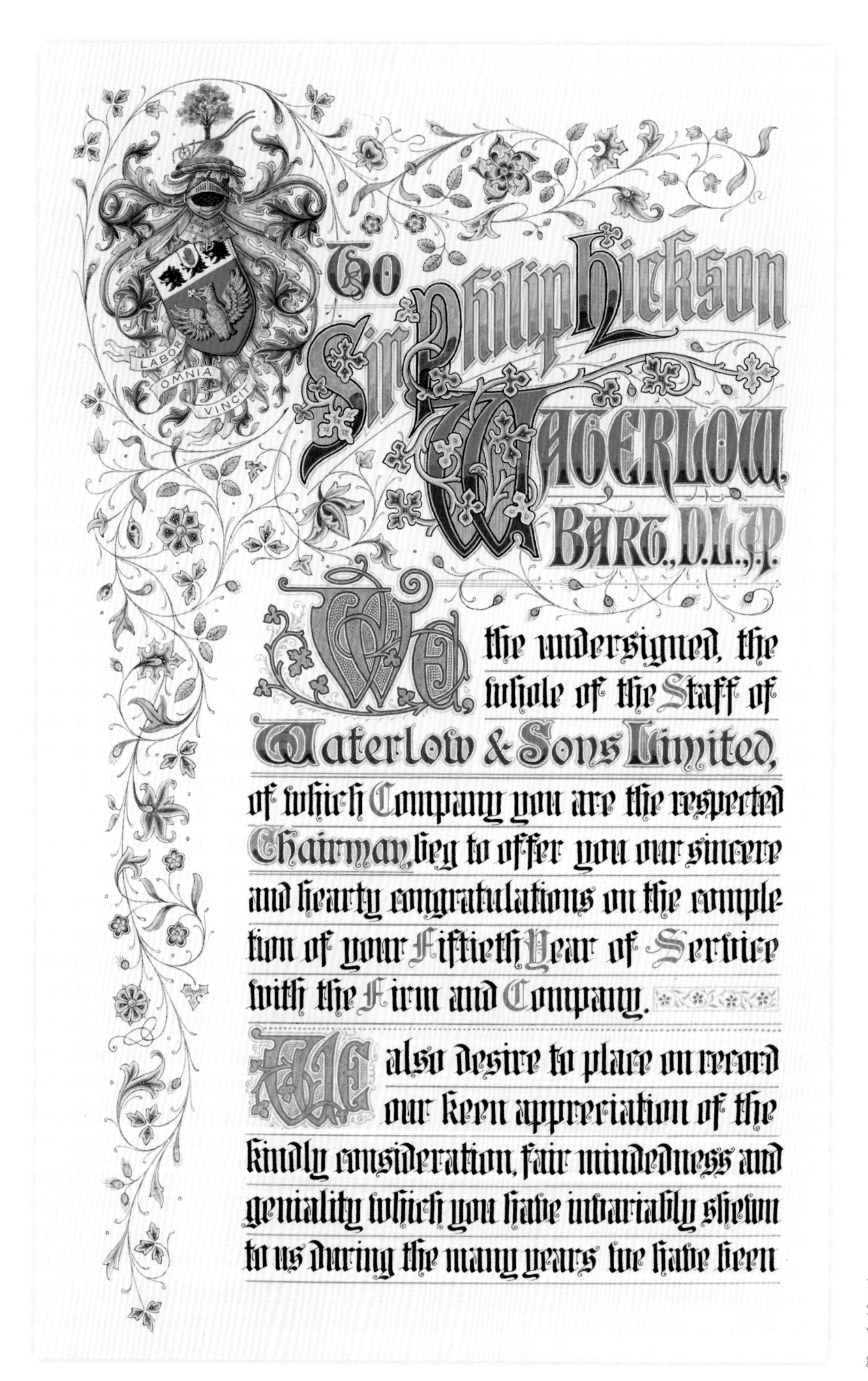

To Sir Philip Hickson Waterlow, Bart., D.L., J.P.

We the undersigned, the whole of the Staff of Waterlow & Sons Limited, of which Company you are the respected Chairman, beg to offer you our sincere and hearty congratulations on the completion of your Fiftieth Year of Service with the Firm and Company.

We also desire to place on record our keen appreciation of the kindly consideration, fair mindedness and geniality which you have invariably shewn to us during the many years we have been

The address to Sir Philip Hickson Waterlow, Bt given in 1914.

associated with you. These attributes, coupled with the quiet confidence with which you have so successfully discharged, for 37 Years, the duties of a most responsible position as Chairman have secured for you the loyalty and affectionate regard of us all and it is to you and your strong personality that the excellent Esprit-de-Corps which obtains in the Company is due.

IN presenting this Address we beg your acceptance of the accompanying Portrait and Sporting Gun with our earnest wish for your long life, happiness, and welfare, and that of your Family.

Name.	Years of Service.
Almond, C.R.	36
Amis, A.	24
Andrews, W.C.	20
Baker, E.T.	16
Barrett, Miss S.	33
Bartlett, G.H.	17
Berry, J.	15
Black, G.H.	5
Black, J.P.	25
Blackaller, C.J.	22
Blott, S.	20
Bodell, T.W.	27
Bond, G.H.	29
Bowyer, G.J.	30
Bowyer, H.G.	22
Bradley, M.J.	33

In 1870 Sir Sydney bought large areas of land in Kent, including the village of Fairseat, part of Stansted, and others near Wrotham and Meopham. In 1887 he built Trosley Towers on the North Downs, within the area that is now Trottiscliffe Country Park.

Sir Philip was born in 1849, London and became a baronet on his father's death in 1906.

He became Chairman of Waterlow & Sons and inherited the Trosley Towers estate from his father. He died in Malling, Kent in 1931, leaving an estate worth £297,000. On his death the Trosley Towers estate was sold and later passed to the Kent County Council.

In 1914 Sir Philip was presented with a striking illumination by all the staff of Waterlow & Sons in celebration of his fifty years of long service to Waterlow & Sons, which included thirty-seven years as Chairman. He was also given a portrait and sporting gun.

A page from the illuminated address.

Lord Chancellor
Sir Thomas Wilde, QS, MP

This is an early illuminated address from 1844. The influence on the unknown illustrator of the design of medieval books of hours can readily be seen. The elegant Old English gothic-style lettering, the side panel and embellished letters used at the start of the paragraphs are all similar in style to those used in previous centuries.

This document, called an 'Inscription' by the donors, is in gratitude from the London Vinegar Makers to Sir Thomas Wilde for acting on their behalf and succeeding in obtaining a relief from the duty on vinegar. Fifteen donors are named. All were vinegar-making businesses from around England. At the head of the list is Sir Robert Burnett & Co. of Vauxhall, a business established in 1770 as Distillers, Rectifiers, Wine and Spirit Merchants and Vinegar Brewers. A Rectifier is someone who blends existing alcohol brands and markets the new flavour under a new brand. Sir Robert Burnett & Co. is still famous for its Burnett's Gin.

Sir Thomas was a lawyer, judge and politician. He was famous as a lawyer for two reasons.

First, he gained notoriety in defending Caroline of Brunswick in 1820. Caroline of Brunswick was the Princess of Wales until 1820 when she became Queen Consort, when her husband became King George IV. As Queen Consort she was due to share her husband's social rank and status but not his political and military powers. However, she had become engaged to be married to Prince George, Prince of Wales before they had met, and George was already illegally married to Maria Fitzherbert. Caroline of Brunswick and Prince George married in 1795 but separated in 1796 after the birth of Princess Charlotte of Wales, their only child. Rumours spread that Princess Caroline had

London xiv June mdcccxliv.

It appearing that in the Bill now before Parliament for repealing the Duty on Vinegar provision is made for the cancellation and return of a portion thereof which has been paid on the stock in hand and yt this provision was obtained by the active interposition and persevering remonstrance of Sir Thomas Wilde Q.S. M.P. on behalf of the Trade.

Resolved unanimously at a meeting of the Vinegar trade holden this day

That the cordial thanks of this Meeting be offered to Sir Thomas Wilde Q.S. M.P. for his persevering and successful exertions in obtaining for the Trade at the hands of Government an act of justice which it is believed would without his interposition have been refused

That Sir Thomas Wilde be requested to accept from the Trade a piece of plate as a testimonial (however inadequate) of their high appreciation of his persevering and effective services in their cause with the following inscription "To Sir Thomas Wilde Q.S. M.P in grateful acknowledgment of important services rendered to the donors.

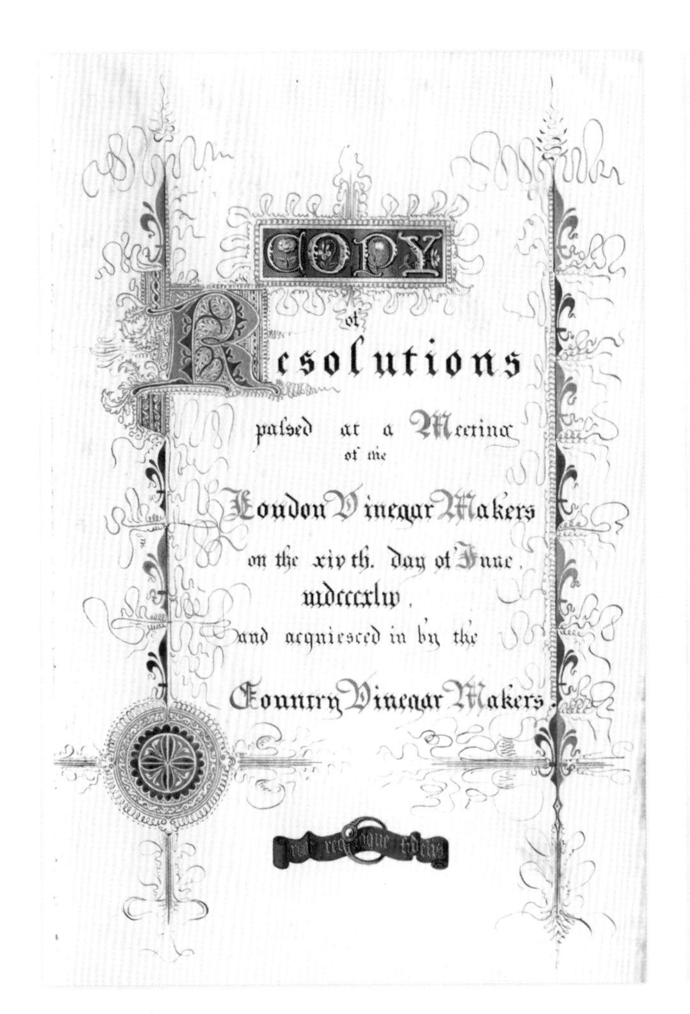

Copy
of
Resolutions
passed at a Meeting
of the
London Vinegar Makers
on the xivth. day of June,
mdcccxliv,
and acquiesced in by the
Country Vinegar Makers

[names of the donors]

Sir Robert Burnett & co. Vauxhall.
Mr. George Clarke Upton on Severn.
Messrs. Forster & Bird Cambridge.
Messrs. Grimble & co. Albany St Regents Pk.
Messrs Hill, Evans & Williams Worcester.
Messrs Hills, Son & Underwood .. Norwich.
Messrs. B. G. Kent & co. Upton on Severn.
Mr. J. P. Osborne Colchester.
Messrs. J. Panter & co. Bristol.
Messrs. Payne & Slee Horsley Down.
Messrs. C. A. & W. Pott Southwark.
Messrs. Purnell & co. Bristol.
Messrs Swann & co. Stockport.
Mrs Waddington Birmingham.
Messrs Willis & Wright ... Old St. London.

The address to Sir Thomas Wilde, QS, MP given in 1844.

lovers and had given birth to an illegitimate child, but an investigation showed no substance in the rumours. Princess Caroline had limited access to her daughter and moved to Italy in 1814 where new rumours began that she had taken her servant as her lover. Back in England, her daughter Princess Charlotte died in childbirth. Prince George requested a divorce but Princess Caroline refused. When he ascended the throne in 1820, Princess Caroline returned to England to claim her right as queen. King George IV tried to obtain a legal divorce through a Bill to Parliament, using evidence of Princess Caroline's infidelity, but it did not succeed. He was not a popular king due to his own immorality, and the public sought political reform, while Princess Caroline had significant support. Unfortunately, she died in 1821.

Secondly, Sir Thomas was a joint founder of the lawyers Wilde Sapte, later to become Denton Wilde Sapte LLP and then SNR Denton.

He became Lord Chancellor in 1850 and was created the 1st Baron Truro. He married twice, his second wife being Mademoiselle d'Este, daughter of Prince Augustus Frederick, Duke of Sussex who was a first cousin of Queen Victoria. Sir Thomas died in 1858 and has a blue plaque to his name in London at 2 Kelvin Avenue, Bowes Park.

Long service
Thomas Hayes

This is an illumination where a number of pages are decorated fully in a delightful Art Nouveau style. The colours are bright and there is a wonderful combination of calligraphy, small detailed pictures, gold highlighting and a connection with a national business with which we, in the UK, are all liable to be familiar: the Co-op.

The presentation was given to Thomas Hayes in 1909 on his eightieth birthday after forty years of service with the Co-operative Wholesale Society (CWS) in Crumpsall, 3 miles north of Manchester. Hayes was a manager in the Biscuit Works, which had opened in 1873, and made biscuits, cakes, sweets, toffee and drugs. The Works boasted being the only eight-hour day biscuit works in England and was progressive in having a cricket club, football club, tennis courts, bowling green, recreation ground, discounted dining room, library, board and card games, and frequent social events such sports days, dances and whist-drives for its staff.

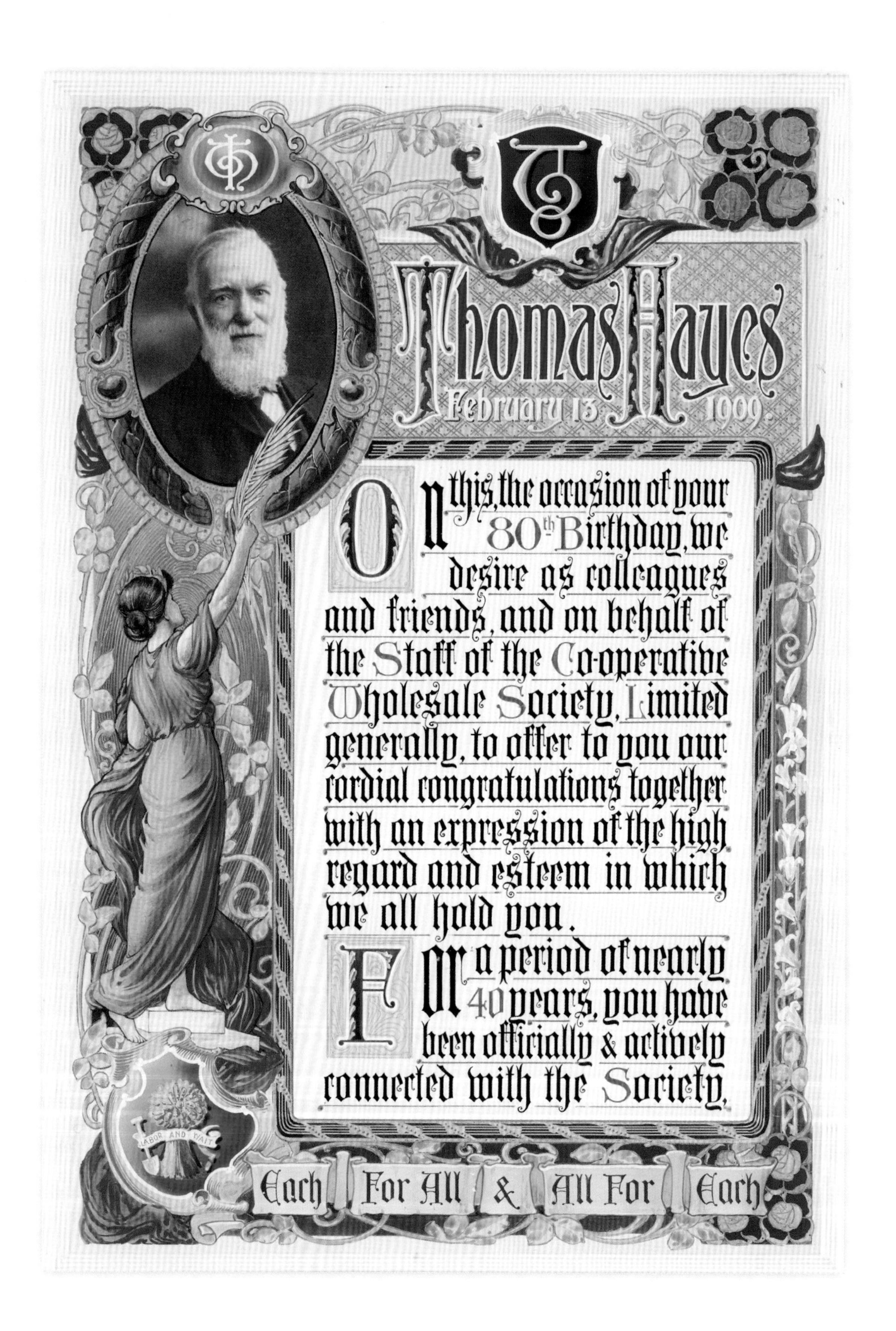

Thomas Hayes
February 13 1909.

On this, the occasion of your 80th Birthday, we desire as colleagues and friends, and on behalf of the Staff of the Co-operative Wholesale Society, Limited generally, to offer to you our cordial congratulations together with an expression of the high regard and esteem in which we all hold you.

For a period of nearly 40 years, you have been officially & actively connected with the Society,

LABOR AND WAIT

Each For All & All For Each

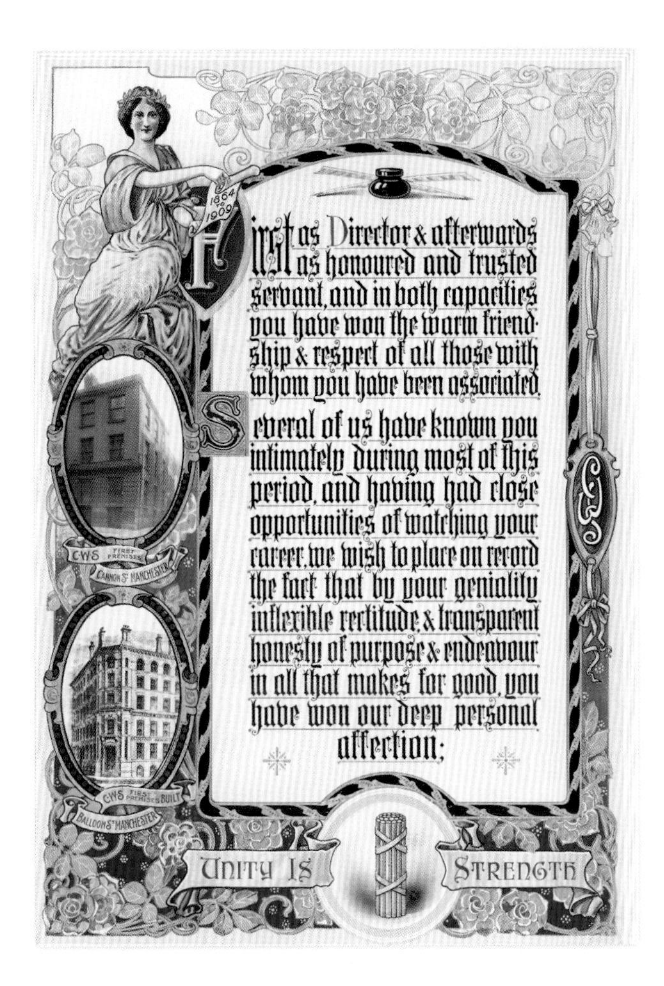

First as Director & afterwards as honoured and trusted servant, and in both capacities you have won the warm friendship & respect of all those with whom you have been associated.

Several of us have known you intimately during most of this period, and having had close opportunities of watching your career, we wish to place on record the fact that by your geniality inflexible rectitude & transparent honesty of purpose & endeavour in all that makes for good, you have won our deep personal affection;

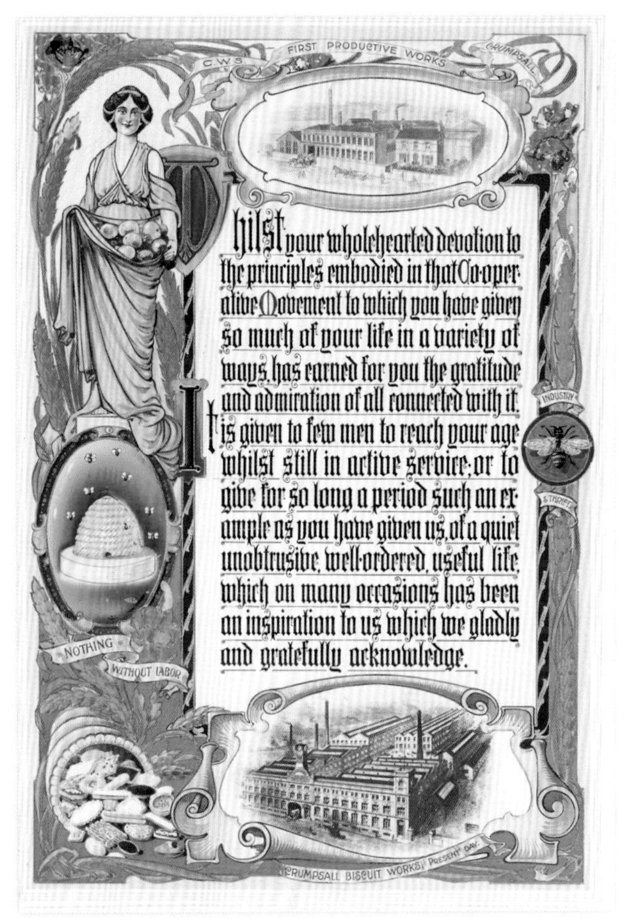

Whilst your wholehearted devotion to the principles embodied in that Co-operative Movement to which you have given so much of your life in a variety of ways, has earned for you the gratitude and admiration of all connected with it.

It is given to few men to reach your age whilst still in active service; or to give for so long a period such an example as you have given us, of a quiet unobtrusive, well-ordered, useful life, which on many occasions has been an inspiration to us which we gladly and gratefully acknowledge.

Pages of the address to Thomas Hayes given in 1909, illuminated by CWS Printing Works, Longsight.

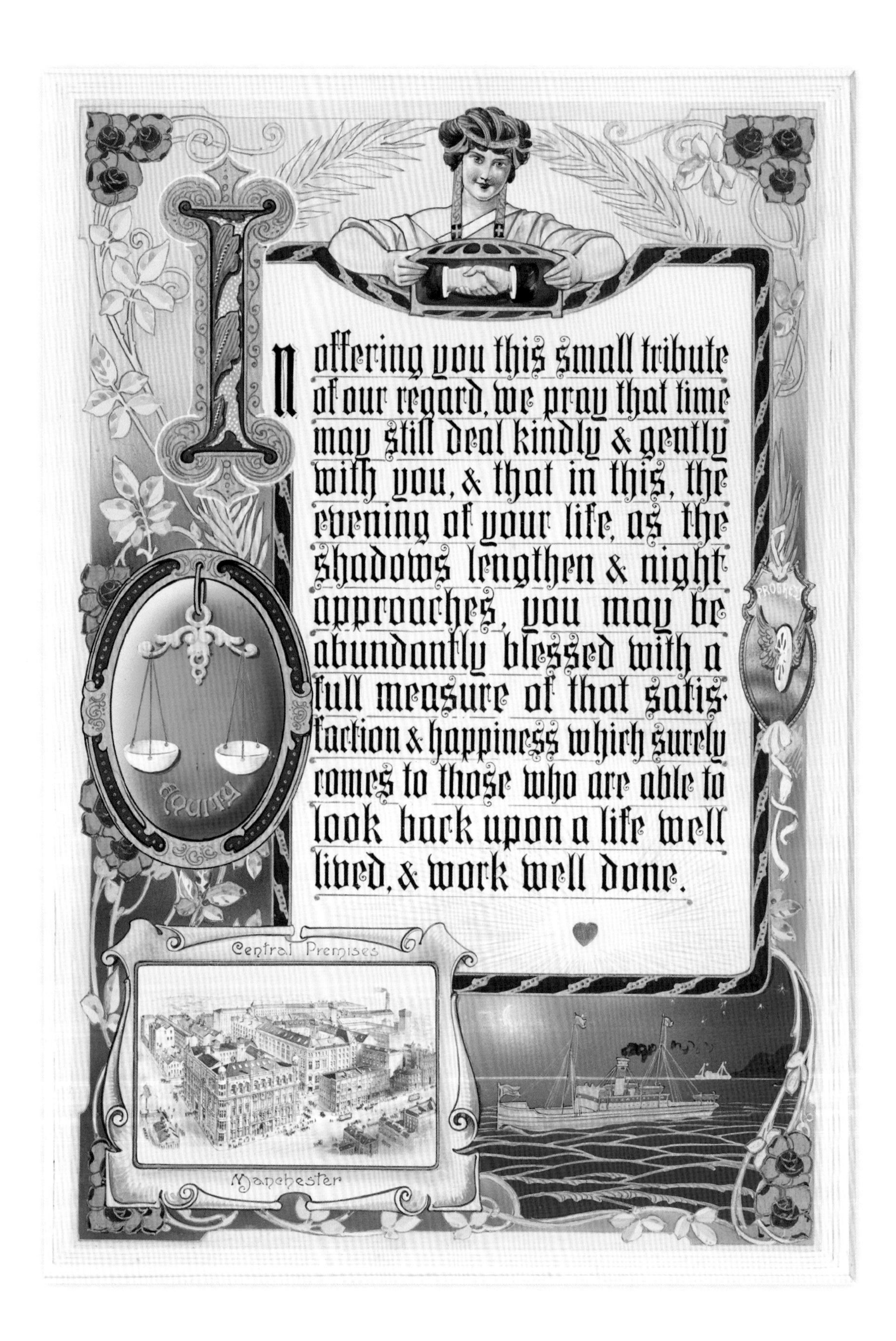

In offering you this small tribute of our regard, we pray that time may still deal kindly & gently with you, & that in this, the evening of your life, as the shadows lengthen & night approaches, you may be abundantly blessed with a full measure of that satisfaction & happiness which surely comes to those who are able to look back upon a life well lived, & work well done.

Hayes had been one of the first members of the Failsworth Industrial Society, formed in 1859 with a co-operative grocery shop. Failsworth is halfway between Oldham and Manchester. Hayes was its first secretary and drew up the rules based on the Rochdale Society of Equitable Pioneers.

The CWS began in 1863 and Failsworth was one of its first shareholders, with Hayes as a part-time director. He also became a director of the Co-operative Newspaper Society and Co-operative Printing Society. Failsworth Industrial Society celebrated its Golden Jubilee in 1909, when it had 10,000 members and forty-three shops. It was a pioneer of a number of new societies, including the United Co-operative Laundries, Manchester and District Funeral Association and United Co-operative Dairies. Failsworth Industrial Society lost its name in 1929 when it merged with New Moston Society.

CHURCH

Clergyman
The Rev. Henry William Burrows

The Rev. Henry William Burrows was the vicar of Christchurch in Albany Street, St Pancras, London until 1878 when he retired and was given, in gratitude, an elegant illuminated presentation by the parishioners.

He was born around 1816 in Malta. He married Maria, seven years his junior, and they had at least four children. They must have been reasonably well-off, as they had four servants. Burrows was appointed a perpetual curate in 1850. He could not call himself a vicar until 1868 and before then had to be referred to as a perpetual curate or parish priest. As a perpetual curate this meant that he could not be removed other than by a bishop, and as a curate he was a 'cure of souls'. Perpetual curates were lower paid than vicars, usually reliant on pay from an endowment, while vicars had the right to a tithe from the parish. The title 'perpetual curate', with a history dating back to the sixteenth century, disappeared in 1868.

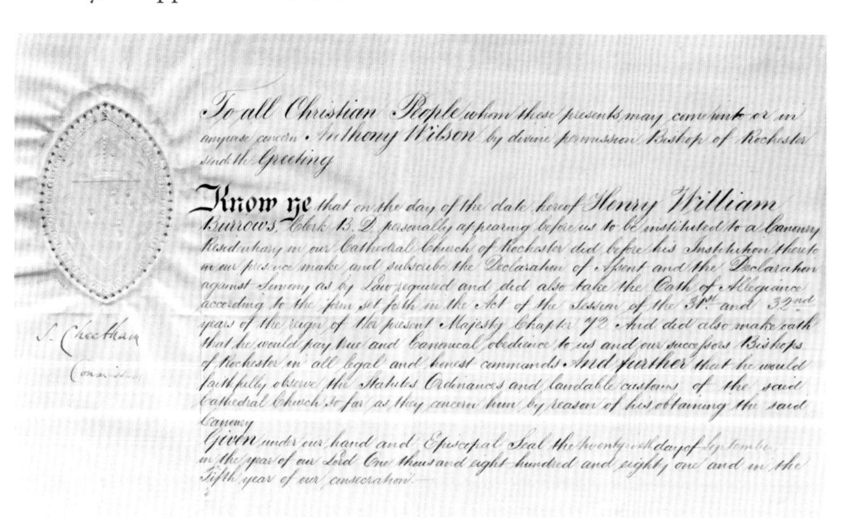

To all Christian People whom these presents may concern or in anywise concern. Anthony Wilson by divine permission Bishop of Rochester send the Greeting

Know ye that on the day of the date hereof Henry William Burrows Clerk B.D. personally appearing before us to be instituted to a Canonry Residentiary in our Cathedral Church of Rochester did before his Institution thereto in our presence make and subscribe the Declaration of Assent and the Declaration against Simony as by Law required and did also take the Oath of Allegiance according to the form set forth in the Act of the Session of the 31st and 32nd years of the reign of Her present Majesty Chapter 72. And did also make oath that he would pay true and Canonical obedience to us and our successors Bishops of Rochester in all legal and honest commands. And further that he would faithfully observe the Statutes Ordinances and laudable customs of the said Cathedral Church so far as they concern him by reason of his obtaining the said Canonry

Given under our hand and Episcopal Seal the twenty-sixth day of September in the year of our Lord One thousand eight hundred and eighty one and in the Fifth year of our consecration

The appointment document of the Rev. Henry William Burrows as a Canon in Rochester Cathedral in 1881.

Page 1 of the address to the Rev. Henry William Burrows given in 1878.

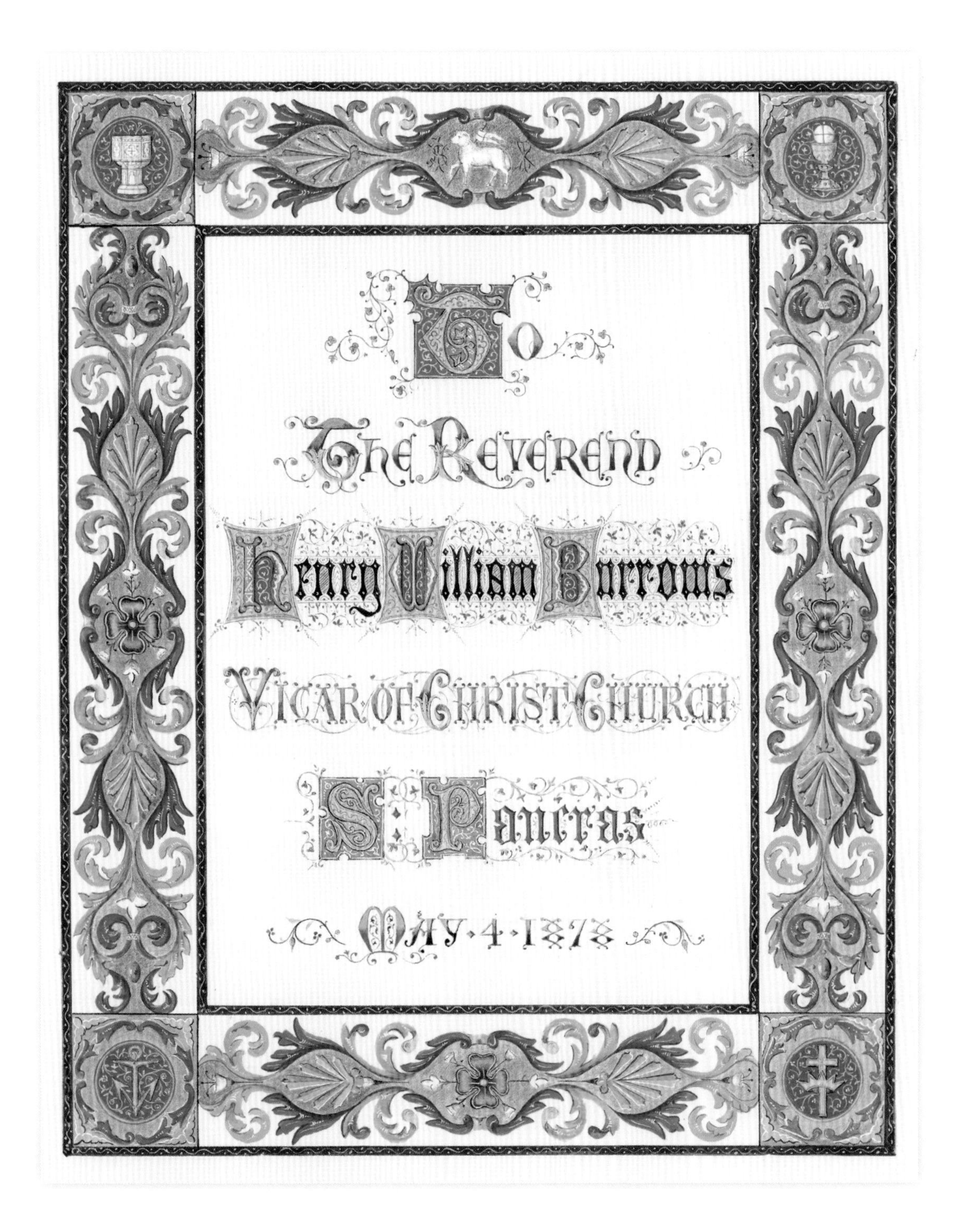
To
The Reverend
Henry William Burrows
Vicar of Christ Church
S. Pancras
May 4 1878

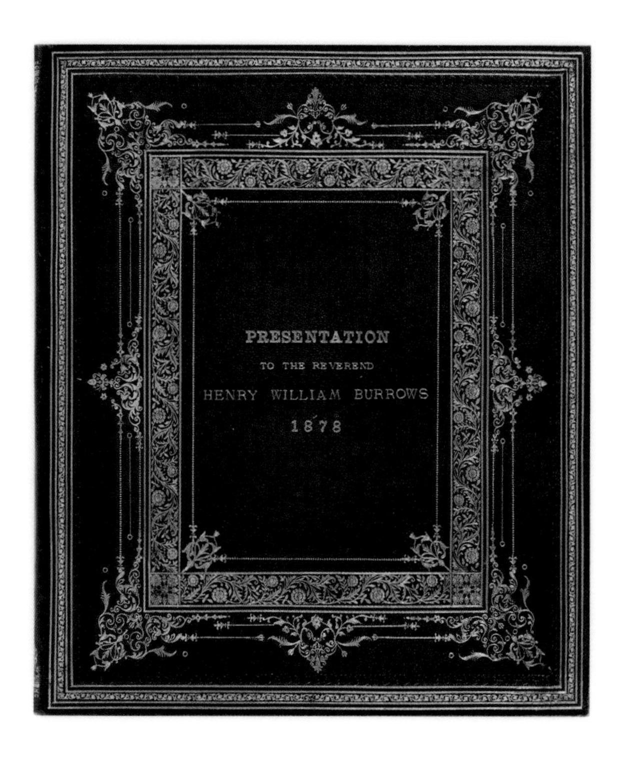

The cover of the address to the Rev. Henry William Burrows given in 1878.

Christchurch was built in 1837 for the parish next to Regent's Park, London, now part of Camden. The church is now St George's Cathedral, London for the Antiochian Orthodox Church. The city of Antioch, near Antakya in southern Turkey, close to the Syrian border, is now in ruins. It was founded in the fourth century BC, and became one of the largest cities in the Roman Empire. Antioch has a long history of Christianity, thought to have begun with St Peter, and the place where followers of Jesus were first called Christians. It was the capital of Syria until the capital was moved to Damascus by the Mamelukes, due to Antioch's earthquakes.

Page 2 of the address to the Rev. Henry William Burrows given in 1878.

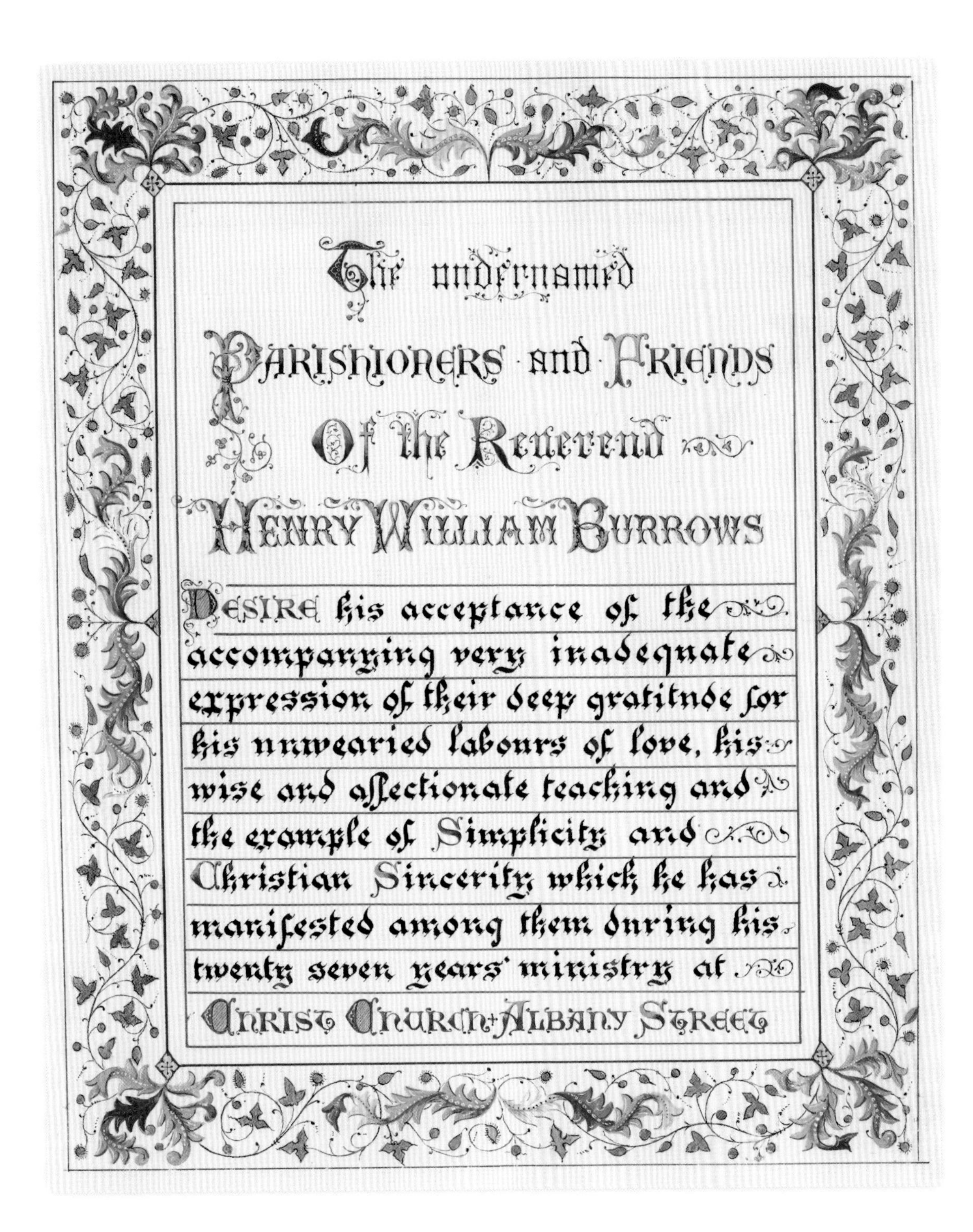

The undernamed
PARISHIONERS and FRIENDS
Of the Reverend
HENRY WILLIAM BURROWS

DESIRE his acceptance of the
accompanying very inadequate
expression of their deep gratitude for
his unwearied labours of love, his
wise and affectionate teaching and
the example of Simplicity and
Christian Sincerity which he has
manifested among them during his
twenty seven years' ministry at
CHRIST CHURCH + ALBANY STREET

A long family tree
Robert John Dobrée

This illuminated address is to Robert John Dobrée, presented in 1875 in gratitude for his 'zealous cooperation' in the purchase and erection of the New Vestry Hall in the parish of St Clement Danes, London. It was signed by the Rev. R.J. Simpson as Chairman on behalf of the Vestry.

The arms of Audray, from which Awdry derives.

St Clement Danes Church is on the Strand, near the Royal Courts of Justice, and is known as the central church of the Royal Air Force. It is thought to have been founded by the Danes in the ninth century, albeit the current building is a restoration of a Sir Christopher Wren building which was bombed in the Second World War.

Pews and chairs in the church include those presented by those connected with the Royal Air Force, including Group Captain Sir Douglas Robert Bader and the Guinea Pig Club, which was a social club for air crew injured in the Second World War who had been patients of Archibald McIndoe, the surgeon at Queen Victoria Hospital in East Grinstead, Sussex. McIndoe was famous for developing treatments of burns with plastic surgery.

This illumination might be quickly dismissed as pleasant and only mildly interesting but for the fascinating family history of the Dobrée family. It illustrates how much of a wider story can be gleaned from a single illuminated address.

Udney Hall.

Dobrée was born close to St-Martin-in-the-Fields, London. He married Caroline Salmon in 1837 and had six children. According to the census, he had a pawnbroking business near Grosvenor Square and lived in Hampstead. Later he lived in Russell Square.

One of Dobrée's sons, Edward, the third child, was born in 1841 at Atkinson Place, Brixton. He was a successful shipping agent and married Fanny Awdry in 1871. They moved to Udney Hall in Teddington, near Hampton Court. Udney Hall had originally been called Teddington Place and had been owned by Sir Charles Duncombe who bought property from the Marquis of Winchester in 1683. Sir Charles was a wealthy banker and was Lord Mayor of London in 1708. He bought many properties, including land in Twickenham which later was owned by Horace Walpole whose residence was Strawberry Hill. Udney Hall was demolished in 1946 and stood in the land now known as Udney Park Gardens.

Edward was keen on family history. He was diligent and thorough in tracing his own and his wife's ancestry. Fanny had a wonderful pedigree, albeit unauthenticated, in that her family tree could be traced back to Norman times. Her ancestry included Sir Fulke

Greville, who served Queen Elizabeth I and King James I in various roles, including Chancellor of the Exchequer. He was given Warwick Castle in 1604. Through his wife, Elizabeth Willoughby, 3rd Baroness Willoughby de Broke, the ancestry can be traced to the Neville family and back to Joan Beaufort, Countess of Westmorland and daughter of John of Gaunt, son of King Edward III.

Edward was interested in establishing his family's right to bear arms and the College of Arms was able to confirm that a grant of arms was awarded to the Dobrée family in 1726, based on historic seals, likely to have come from France.

Edward could trace his father's ancestry, through the Dobrée name, back through Guernsey to France.

The arms of Dobrée.

The first Dobrées to settle in Guernsey arrived in the middle of the sixteenth century, around 1560, from Normandy, as Huguenots, so as to be able to follow the Protestant religion. Another reason for moving to Guernsey comes from a story in their family history. It is believed that Jehan Dobrée was in the service of Gabriel de Lorges, the 1st Earl of Montgomery who, unfortunately, mortally wounded King Henry II in a jousting tournament in 1559 when a splinter from his lance went through the king's eye. He fled to Guernsey as he was friends with Sir Thomas Leighton, the Governor of Guernsey.

It is believed that Jehan followed de Lorges to Guernsey. His wife was Michelle, daughter of John Le Mesurier, a magistrate on Guernsey. (Note that John Le Mesurier, the twentieth-century actor, famous in the television show *Dad's Army*, was born John Elton Le Mesurier

The arms of Le Mesurier.

Halliley, with Le Mesurier being the maiden name of his mother, whose family came from the Channel Isles. It seems likely that his ancestry can be traced back to be closely connected to the Dobrée family.)

The Dobrées did well in Guernsey, but some of them returned to France. One descendent, Thomas Dobrée, was an avid and extreme collector and created a palace to house his collections in Nantes (only completed after his death). His objects included books, paintings, coins, medals engravings and sculpture. Thomas died in 1895 and left his palace and collections to the Département de Loire-Inférieure which then called it the Musée Thomas Dobrée, and which still exists today

Many of the Dobrée descendants migrated to England and also did well. For instance, Samuel Dobrée established a merchant and shipping business in Guernsey known as Samuel Dobrée & Son. The Bank of Samuel Dobree & Son was established and lasted for more than 200 years, operating from offices in 7 Moorgate, London. Another Dobrée, Bonamy Dobrée, was Governor of the Bank of England from 1859–61.

Thomas Dobrée.

Pages 1 and 2 of the address to Robert John Dobrée given in 1875, illuminated by Peters & Co., Warwick House, Gray's Inn.

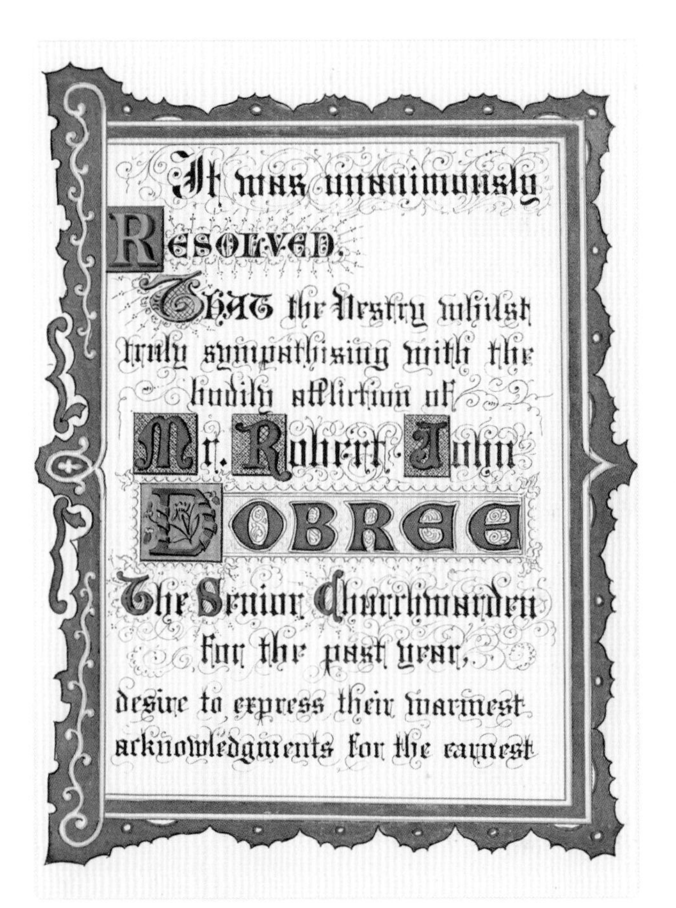

It was unanimously
RESOLVED,
THAT the Vestry whilst
truly sympathising with the
bodily affliction of
Mr. Robert John
DOBREE
The Senior Churchwarden
for the past year,
desire to express their warmest
acknowledgments for the earnest

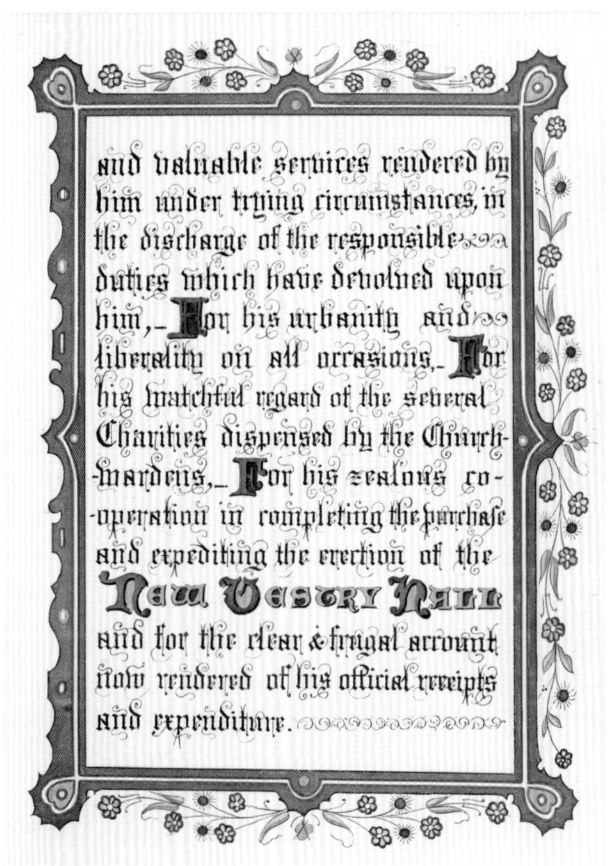

and valuable services rendered by
him under trying circumstances, in
the discharge of the responsible
duties which have devolved upon
him,– For his urbanity and
liberality on all occasions,– For
his watchful regard of the several
Charities dispensed by the Church-
-wardens,– For his zealous co-
-operation in completing the purchase
and expediting the erection of the
NEW VESTRY HALL
and for the clear & frugal account
now rendered of his official receipts
and expenditure.

Pages 3 and 4 of the address to Robert John Dobrée given in 1875, illuminated by Peters & Co., Warwick House, Gray's Inn.

Sunday school teacher
William Harrison

This is a small but beautiful illumination that begins with a skilfully painted coat of arms.

The presentation is actually to The Misses Harrison and William Harrison of Arlington House, Knaresborough. It was the closure of the Forest Lane Mission Room in Knaresborough in 1890 that led the members to give the presentation, in gratitude for the Harrisons' service to the Mission Room.

William Harrison and his sisters Charlotte and Temperance lived at Arlington House on Forest Moor Road. They ran the Forest Lane Sunday School until Charlotte's death in 1902, when the school was transferred to St Andrew's Church. The school was subsequently sold to raise funds for a new church.

Coat of arms within the illuminated address to William Harrison given in 1890.

William, Charlotte and Temperance were the children of Thomas Harrison, a banker. The family were religious and supportive of education and the poor. Charlotte opened a Sunday School in 1854 with the support of her father.

Knaresborough is a small market town within the Borough of Harrogate, North Yorkshire. It has a Norman castle where, in 1210 it is believed that King John distributed the first alms to the poor at the Maundy service. The Maundy service developed from the ceremony of washing feet of the poor, begun when Jesus washed the feet of his disciples on the eve of his Crucifixion. Later, kings and

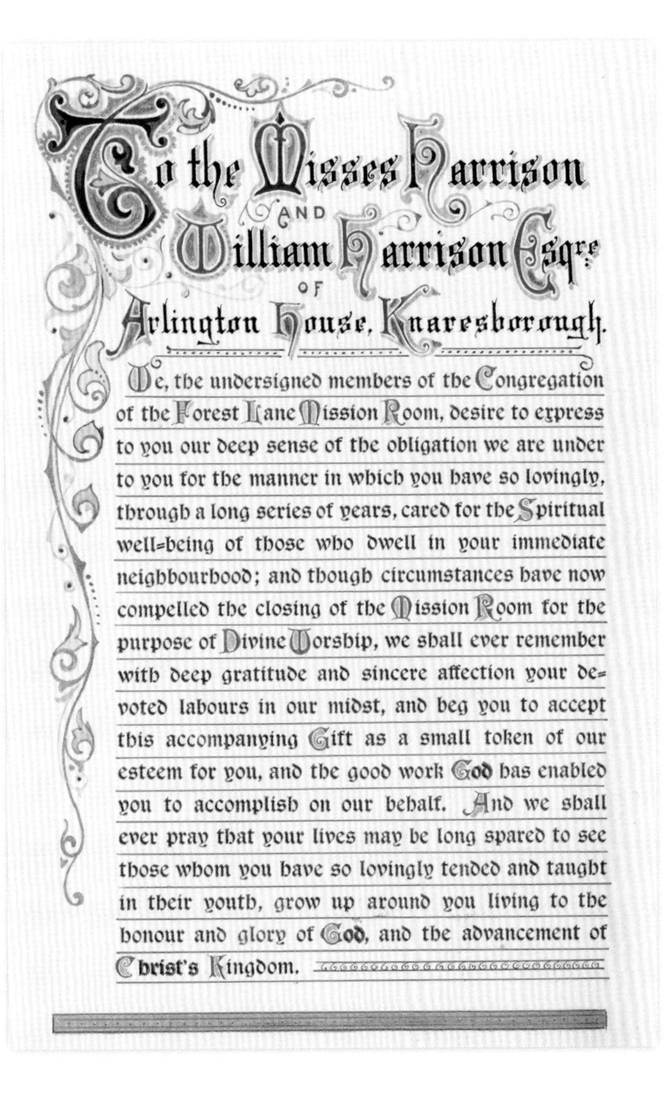

To the Misses Harrison
AND
William Harrison Esqre
OF
Arlington House, Knaresborough.

We, the undersigned members of the Congregation of the Forest Lane Mission Room, desire to express to you our deep sense of the obligation we are under to you for the manner in which you have so lovingly, through a long series of years, cared for the Spiritual well-being of those who dwell in your immediate neighbourhood; and though circumstances have now compelled the closing of the Mission Room for the purpose of Divine Worship, we shall ever remember with deep gratitude and sincere affection your devoted labours in our midst, and beg you to accept this accompanying Gift as a small token of our esteem for you, and the good work God has enabled you to accomplish on our behalf. And we shall ever pray that your lives may be long spared to see those whom you have so lovingly tended and taught in their youth, grow up around you living to the honour and glory of God, and the advancement of Christ's Kingdom.

The illuminated address.

queens repeated the practice of giving gifts to the poor and some also washed the feet of the poor. Maundy sets of money comprising 1*d*, 2*d*, 3*d* and 4*d* were first dated from 1670 (but there was an earlier undated set). Currently, it is practice for two purses to be handed out, one containing Maundy money to the value of the same number of pence as the monarch's age, and the other with a £5 coin and a 50p coin.

CIVIC DUTY

Public servant
Alderman Alfred John Knott

Alfred John Knott was an alderman, a chief magistrate and Mayor of Grimsby. He was presented with a wonderful illuminated presentation in 1931 for his services as Mayor.

An alderman is a high-ranking member of a borough or county council. The name derives from elder man, a chief noble who presided over a shire. The name mostly disappeared in 1974 under the Local Government Act 1972, except for London boroughs where the position was abolished in 1978. However, the City of London still has aldermen, elected for each ward by the public. Only people who have been an alderman and a sheriff can be a candidate for the Lord Mayor of the City of London.

Knott was born in Grimsby in around 1865 and stayed most of his working life in the area, working as a fish merchant. He died in 1938. His son Claude, born in 1891, also worked as a fish merchant before

Page 1 of the address to Alderman Alfred John Knott given in 1931.

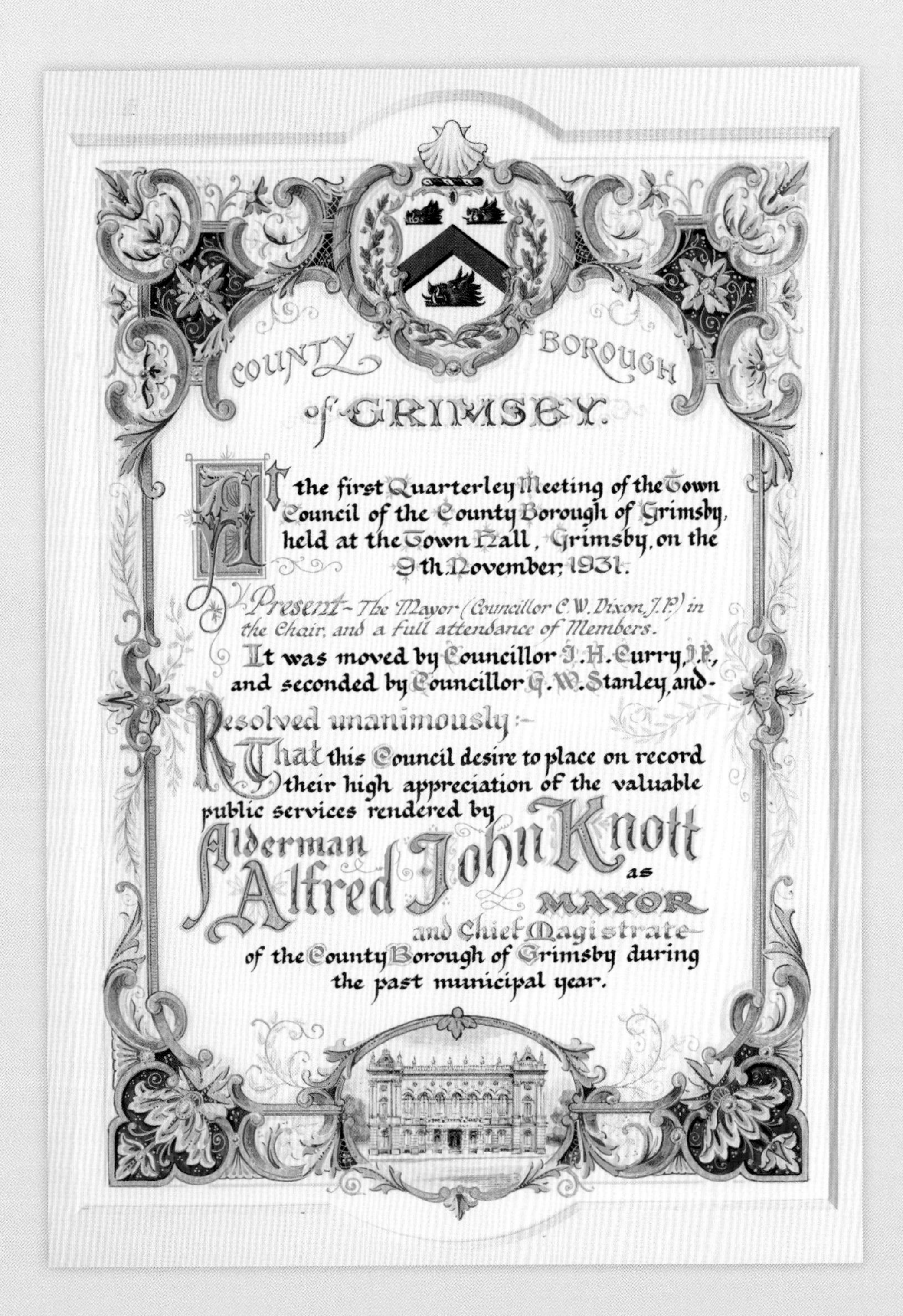

County Borough of Grimsby.

At the first Quarterley Meeting of the Town Council of the County Borough of Grimsby, held at the Town Hall, Grimsby, on the 9th November, 1931.

Present – The Mayor (Councillor C.W. Dixon, J.P.) in the Chair, and a full attendance of Members.

It was moved by Councillor J.H. Curry, J.P., and seconded by Councillor G.W. Stanley, and –

Resolved unanimously:–

That this Council desire to place on record their high appreciation of the valuable public services rendered by

Alderman Alfred John Knott as MAYOR and Chief Magistrate of the County Borough of Grimsby during the past municipal year.

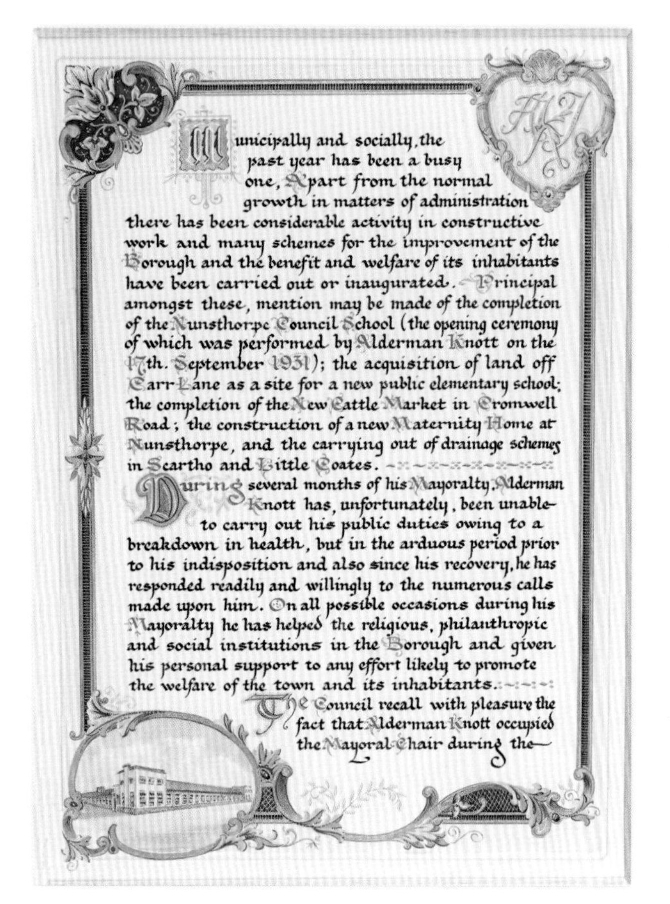

Municipally and socially, the past year has been a busy one. Apart from the normal growth in matters of administration there has been considerable activity in constructive work and many schemes for the improvement of the Borough and the benefit and welfare of its inhabitants have been carried out or inaugurated. Principal amongst these, mention may be made of the completion of the Nunsthorpe Council School (the opening ceremony of which was performed by Alderman Knott on the 17th. September 1931); the acquisition of land off Carr Lane as a site for a new public elementary school; the completion of the New Cattle Market in Cromwell Road; the construction of a new Maternity Home at Nunsthorpe, and the carrying out of drainage schemes in Scartho and Little Coates.

During several months of his Mayoralty, Alderman Knott has, unfortunately, been unable to carry out his public duties owing to a breakdown in health, but in the arduous period prior to his indisposition and also since his recovery, he has responded readily and willingly to the numerous calls made upon him. On all possible occasions during his Mayoralty he has helped the religious, philanthropic and social institutions in the Borough and given his personal support to any effort likely to promote the welfare of the town and its inhabitants.

The Council recall with pleasure the fact that Alderman Knott occupied the Mayoral Chair during the

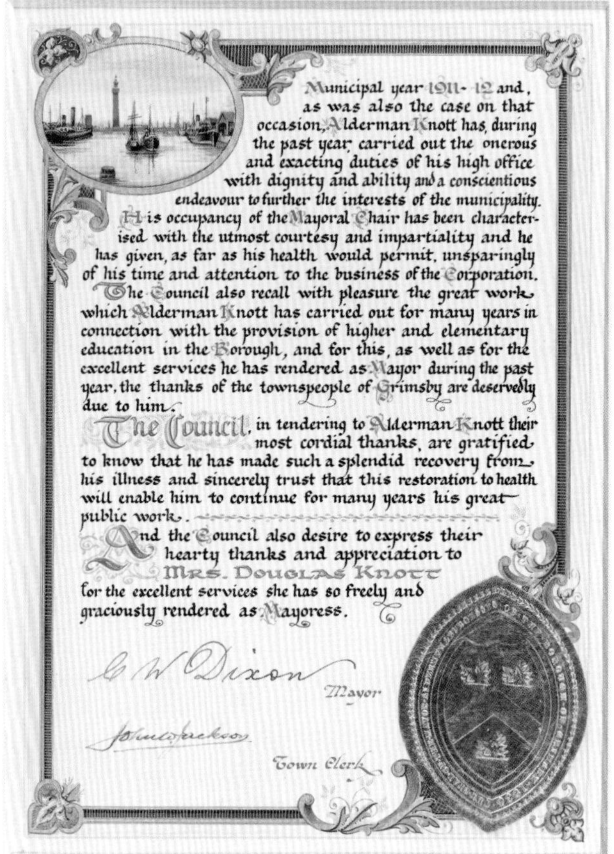

Municipal year 1911-12 and, as was also the case on that occasion, Alderman Knott has, during the past year, carried out the onerous and exacting duties of his high office with dignity and ability and a conscientious endeavour to further the interests of the municipality. His occupancy of the Mayoral Chair has been characterised with the utmost courtesy and impartiality and he has given, as far as his health would permit, unsparingly of his time and attention to the business of the Corporation.

The Council also recall with pleasure the great work which Alderman Knott has carried out for many years in connection with the provision of higher and elementary education in the Borough, and for this, as well as for the excellent services he has rendered as Mayor during the past year, the thanks of the townspeople of Grimsby are deservedly due to him.

The Council, in tendering to Alderman Knott their most cordial thanks, are gratified to know that he has made such a splendid recovery from his illness and sincerely trust that this restoration to health will enable him to continue for many years his great public work.

And the Council also desire to express their hearty thanks and appreciation to MRS. DOUGLAS KNOTT for the excellent services she has so freely and graciously rendered as Mayoress.

C W Dixon
Mayor

Town Clerk

Pages 2 and 3 of the address to Alderman Alfred John Knott given in 1931.

joining the army with the Lincolnshire Regiment in the Special Reserve Battalion (No. 3). Claude married Dorothy Compton in 1919 in Middlesex and died in 1960. Grimsby was a major sea port, having the largest fishing fleet in the world by the mid-twentieth century, but the fishing industry declined in the 1970s due to the Cod Wars.

Lord Mayor of Cardiff
Alderman James Hellyer, JP

Alderman James Hellyer retired from the roles of Lord Mayor and Chief Magistrate of Cardiff in 1942. This occurred in the midst of the Second World War and his bright and attractive illuminated address makes reference to war effort fund-raising of £4.5m in Cardiff Warships Week, the Dig for Victory Exhibition and the Stay at Home Holidays campaign. The address also notes his hospitality to the Princess Mary, the Princess Royal and Princess Alice, the Duchess of Gloucester, both aunts of Queen Elizabeth II.

The address illustrates the splendid arms of Cardiff. These were granted in 1906, but with subsequent amendments. The shield shows a red dragon next to a leek, and the dragon is holding a standard with

Page 1 of the address to Alderman James Hellyer, JP given in 1942.

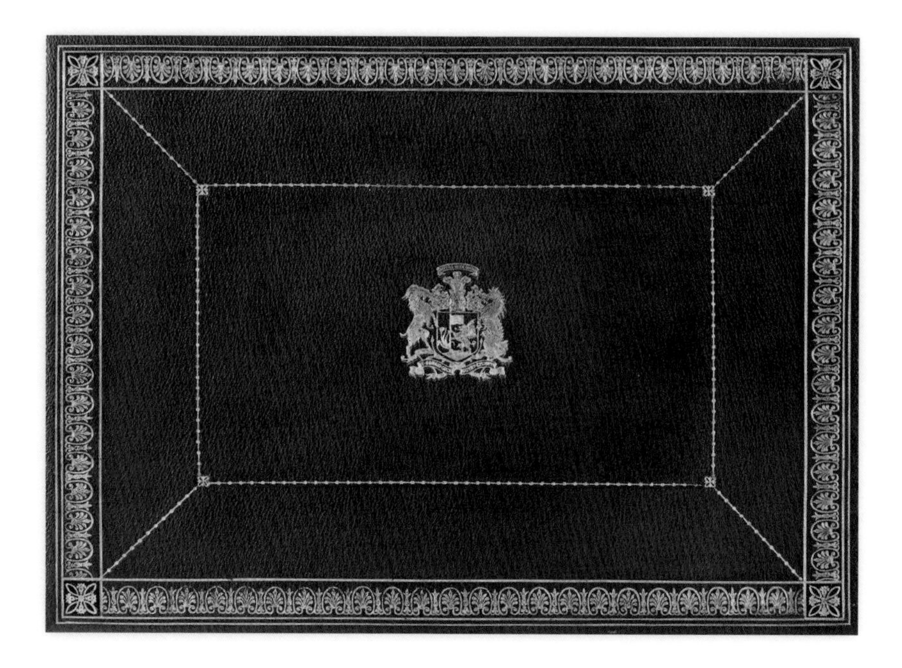

arms thought to be of the last Prince of Glamorgan. Under the shield is a motto meaning the red dragon will lead the way.

The crest at the top has a Tudor Rose on three ostrich feathers sitting on a crown. The motto above the crest means awake, it is day.

The animals (supporters) either side are a goat, an emblem of the Welsh mountains, and a seahorse, to represent the sea and commerce to Cardiff port. There are five small photos depicting Cardiff in 1942: the City Hall, University College, HMS *Cardiff*, Jubilee Cottages Ely and allotments to represent the Dig For Victory Campaign.

HMS *Cardiff* was the second of four ships to bear this name. The pictured ship was in use from 1917–46. She participated in the Second Battle of Heligoland in 1917 and thereafter in the Baltic to support the anti-Bolshevik campaign in the Russian Civil War. In the Second World War she was a patrol ship within the northern patrol seeking German ships and later became a gunnery training ship. She was broken up for scrap in 1946.

Pages 2, 3 and 4 of the address to Alderman James Hellyer, JP given in 1942.

CITY HALL · CARDIFF

CITY OF CARDIFF

At the Annual Meeting of the Council of the City of Cardiff, held at the City Hall, Cathays Park, Cardiff, on Monday, the 9th day of November, 1942, it was Moved by Alderman Purnell, seconded by Councillor Robson, supported by the Deputy Lord Mayor (Councillor A.J. Williams, J.P.), and

Resolved Unanimously

That, upon the Retirement of

Alderman James Hellyer, J.P.

from the position of

Lord Mayor and Chief Magistrate

UNIVERSITY COLLEGE

The Council also desire to express to the Lady Mayoress (Mrs. James Hellyer) their sincere thanks for the dignity and charm which have characterised the performance of her duties as Lady Mayoress and for the support which she has rendered to her husband during his Lord Mayoralty.

That this Resolution be suitably engrossed (on vellum) sealed with the corporate seal, signed by the Lord Mayor and the Town Clerk, and presented to Alderman Hellyer, together with replica of the Lord Mayoral Badge, and that a similar replica be presented to Mrs. Hellyer.

In Witness whereof the Common Seal of the Lord Mayor, Aldermen & Citizens of the City of Cardiff was hereunto affixed the 9th day of November, 1942, in the presence of:—

James Griffiths — Lord Mayor

Deputy Town Clerk

'DIG FOR VICTORY' CAMPAIGN · 1942

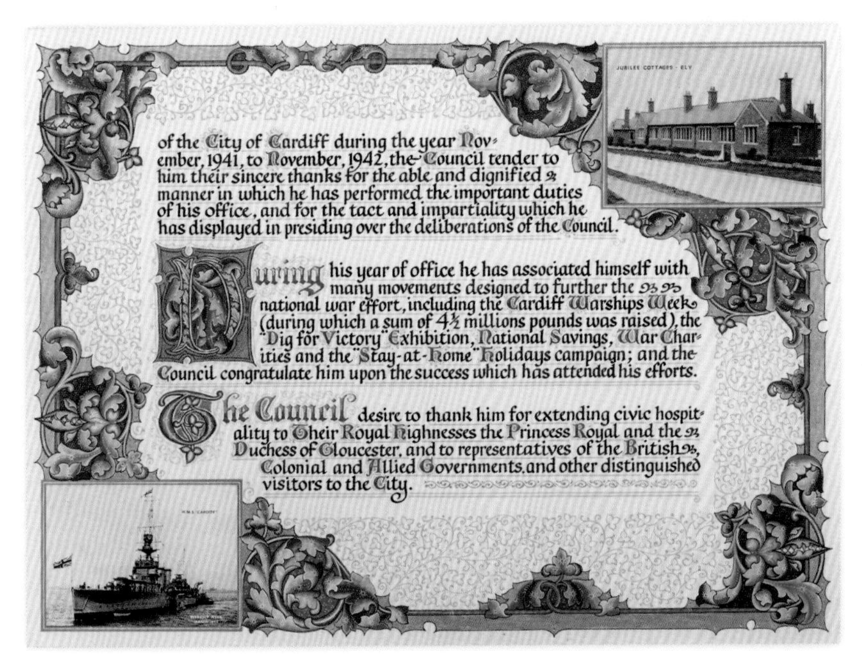

of the City of Cardiff during the year November, 1941, to November, 1942, the Council tender to him their sincere thanks for the able and dignified manner in which he has performed the important duties of his office, and for the tact and impartiality which he has displayed in presiding over the deliberations of the Council.

During his year of office he has associated himself with many movements designed to further the national war effort, including the Cardiff Warships Week (during which a sum of 4½ millions pounds was raised), the "Dig for Victory" Exhibition, National Savings, War Charities and the "Stay-at-Home" Holidays campaign; and the Council congratulate him upon the success which has attended his efforts.

The Council desire to thank him for extending civic hospitality to Their Royal Highnesses the Princess Royal and the Duchess of Gloucester, and to representatives of the British, Colonial and Allied Governments, and other distinguished visitors to the City.

JUBILEE COTTAGES · ELY

H.M.S. CARDIFF

Watch Committee Chairman
Alderman William Hughes

In 1937 Alderman William Hughes was presented with a colourful illuminated address in gratitude for his service as Chairman of the Watch Committee of Salford. He had been a member of the committee since 1895 and had been Chairman since 1920.

The illumination is enhanced by four neat vignettes of municipal buildings: Salford Town Hall in Bexley Square, Salford; Police 'A' Division Headquarters in Regent Road, Salford; Pendleton Police Station, Salford; Police 'C' Division Headquarters in Park Lane, Broughton, Salford.

A Watch Committee was a committee within the local authority that was given the power to oversee local policing, until it was replaced by the introduction of police authorities.

Hughes was given the Freedom of the City in 1941 after serving fifty years as a councillor. There had been only six prior recipients of the Freedom, one of whom was the Rt Hon. David Lloyd George, OM, MP.

Hughes had also been Mayor of Salford from 1919–20. In addition, in 1941 he achieved his seventieth year of membership of the Methodist Church. He had been a Superintendent at the church, which had involved fundraising for a new church and school. It had been his service in the Enys Street Methodist Church that had led a deputation of miners in Pendleton (an inner city suburb of Salford) to approach him to stand as a Liberal working-man's candidate and civil spokesman in the 1891 elections. He supported the miners when they went on strike by suspending his own work and providing a soup kitchen for seventeen weeks.

Page 1 of the address to Alderman William Hughes given in 1937, illuminated by Alan Tabor.

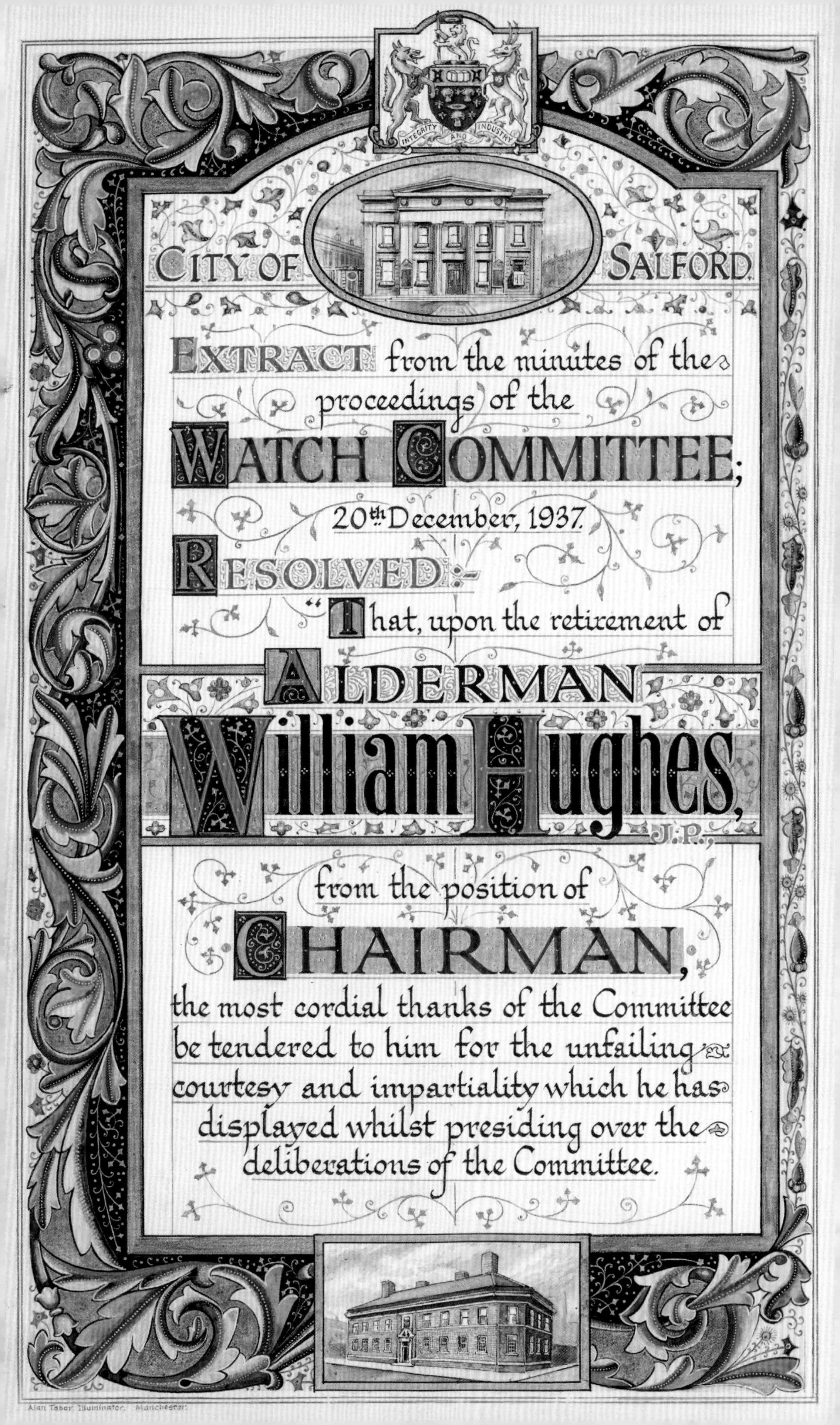
INTEGRITY AND INDUSTRY
CITY OF SALFORD
EXTRACT from the minutes of the proceedings of the
WATCH COMMITTEE;
20th December, 1937.
RESOLVED:-
"That, upon the retirement of
ALDERMAN
William Hughes,
J.P.,
from the position of
CHAIRMAN,
the most cordial thanks of the Committee be tendered to him for the unfailing courtesy and impartiality which he has displayed whilst presiding over the deliberations of the Committee.
Alan Tabor, Illuminator, Manchester.

Page 2 of the address to Alderman William Hughes given in 1937, illuminated by Alan Tabor.

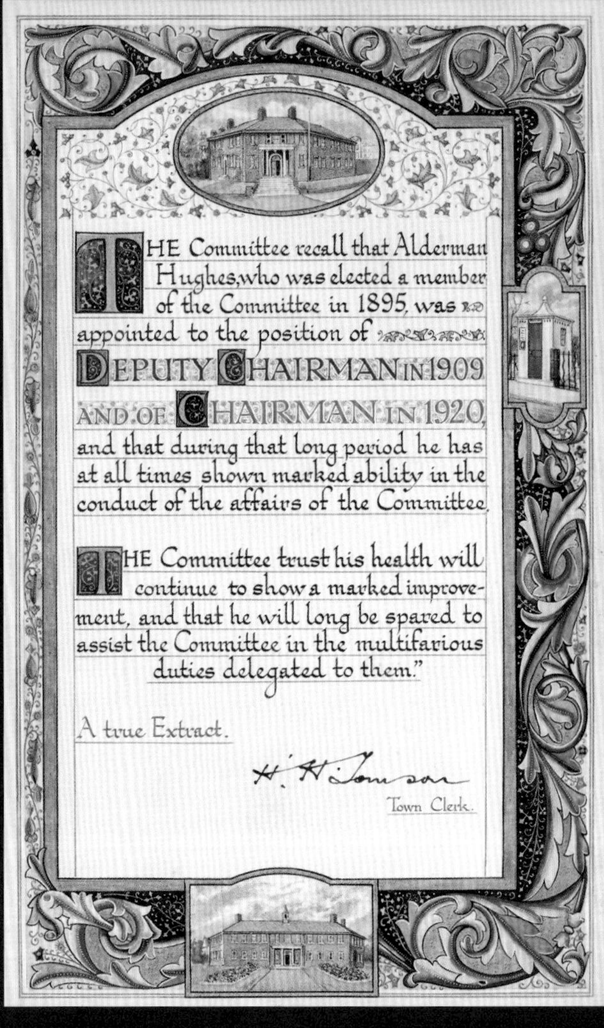

THE Committee recall that Alderman Hughes, who was elected a member of the Committee in 1895, was appointed to the position of DEPUTY CHAIRMAN IN 1909 AND OF CHAIRMAN IN 1920, and that during that long period he has at all times shown marked ability in the conduct of the affairs of the Committee.

THE Committee trust his health will continue to show a marked improvement, and that he will long be spared to assist the Committee in the multifarious duties delegated to them."

A true Extract.

Town Clerk.

Alan Tabor was the skilled illuminator of the Watch Committee illuminated address. He was based in Manchester and was a commercial artist describing himself as an illuminator. He was widely used. Tabor designed many long service certificates for companies in Lancashire and produced the calligraphy and artwork for a handwritten book, *A Christmas Carol* by Charles Dickens in prose that was published by George Harrap & Co. in 1916. There are examples of his work held by the National Trust in Lanhydrock, Cornwall, Wightwick Manor, West Midlands and Nuffield Place, Oxfordshire.

Chairman of the Library Committee
Athro Charles Knight

Some people spend so much time working for their clubs, societies and committees that perhaps they have less time for their families. Athro Charles Knight appears to be such a person. He was married to Violet Evelyn Turner and they had one daughter. It seems that he preferred to be known as Charles.

Knight went to Dulwich College, studied at Lincoln's Inn and rose to become a Senior Partner in the solicitors Mackrell, Ward & Knight. He lived in Herne Place, Sunningdale, Berkshire in a thirty-two-room mansion that later became a recording studio run by Eddie Hardin who had been in the Spencer Davis Group. Now it consists of apartments.

Knight was a London Justice of the Peace, Fellow of the Society of Antiquaries and a Fellow of the Royal Historical Society. He was a member of London City Corporation from 1916, one of the Lieutenants of the City, Deputy of the Ward of Cheap and an Under Sheriff. He was also a member of the London County Council, representing the Municipal Reform Party for Islington North. He was Chairman of the Guildhall Library. For his year of service on the Guildhall Library Committee, in 1923, he was given a lovely illuminated address and an old English silver tea service!

Knight was a founder (in 1914) and President (in 1927) of the City Livery Club. The club's original meeting place was at De Keyser's Royal Hotel. Sir Polydore de Keyser was a Belgian waiter who came to London to make his fortune. He built the 400-room hotel in 1874 near Blackfriars, on the site that later became Unilever House. The hotel hosted many Guildhall banquets and was the first meeting place of the City Livery Club before being demolished in 1930. Having received

British nationality, Sir Polydore became Lord Mayor of London in 1887, the first Catholic to be elected to the office since the Reformation.

Knight was on the Council of the London Topographical Society, on the Executive Committee of the London Society, a director of the French Hospital and Deputy Governor of The Honourable The Irish Society. He was a chairman of the City Police Committee, Commissioner in England for Australia, India, Canada and Africa, a Freeman of the City of London from 1912 and was Master of the Worshipful Companies of Fletchers, Scriveners, Tallow Chandlers and Barber Surgeons. He was also a Commander of the Most Venerable Order of the Hospital of Saint John of Jerusalem.

Knight has work published as well, including *Cordwainer Ward in the City of London, its History and Topography*, and *The Tallow Chandlers' Company: its Origin, a sketch of its History*. He died at the age of seventy-nine. There is a stained glass window in his memory in St Lawrence Jewry church.

The address to Athro Charles Knight given in 1923.

FACTIS NON VERBIS

To

A. Charles Knight, Esq.,

one of

His Majesty's Justices of the Peace for the County of London, Fellow of the Society of Antiquaries, & of the Royal Historical Society-Chairman of the Guildhall Library Committee, 1926.

DOMINE DIRIGE NOS

Newton.
MAYOR.

Resolved:-

That the Guildhall Library Committee in concluding their work for the year sincerely thank their esteemed & popular Chairman for the able manner in which he has discharged his duties and desire to place on record that on being unanimously elected, he has devoted much time & attention to the affairs of the Committee and ask him to accept as a souvenir of his Chairmanship the accompanying Old English Silver Tea Service & in thanking him for his invariable courtesy to every member & for his impartiality in the Chair, express the hope that he may long continue to give to the Corporation and the Citizens the benefit of his experienced services.

Bell

Town Clerk of the City of London.

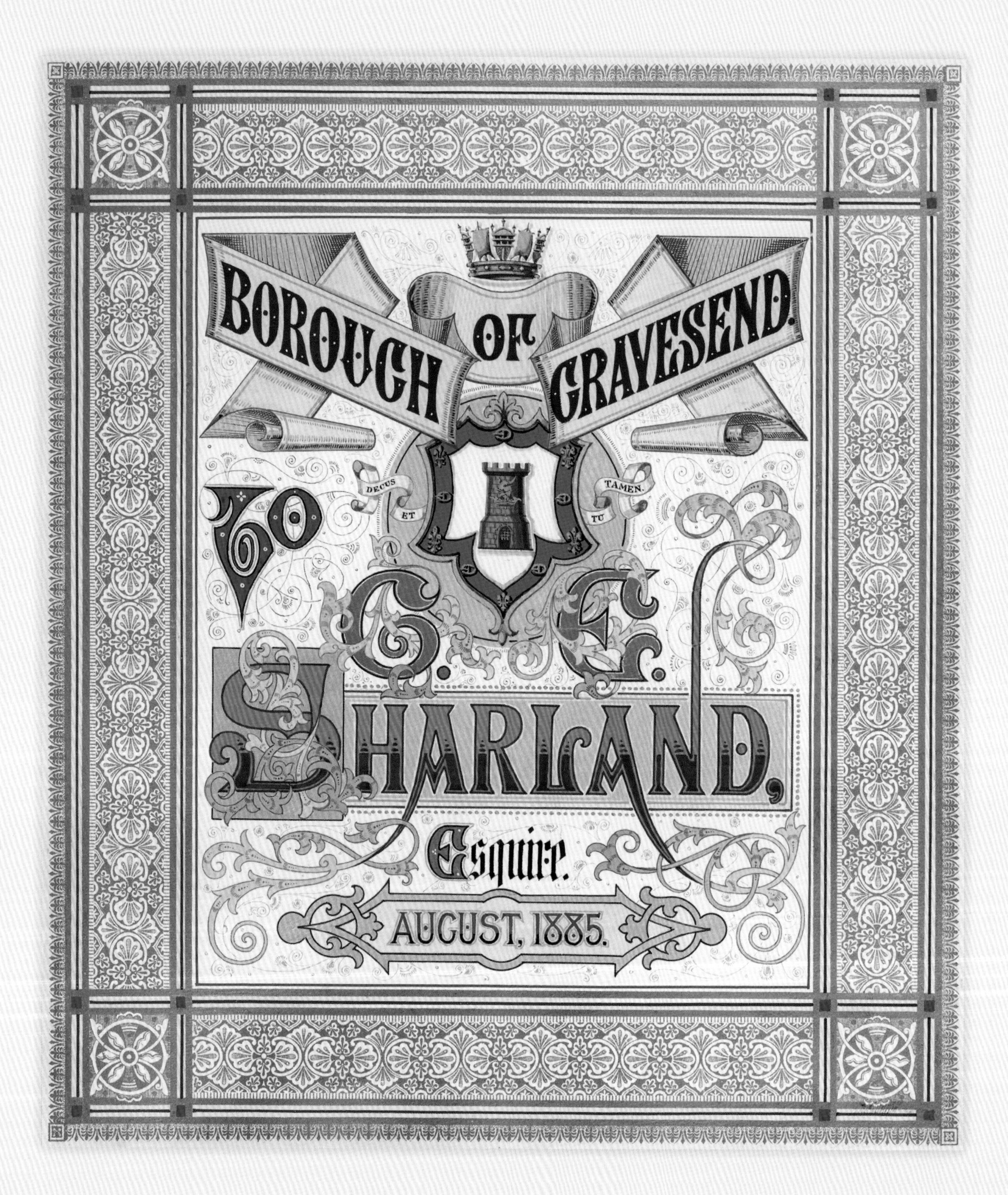
BOROUGH OF GRAVESEND.
DECUS ET TAMEN TU
TO
G. E. SHARLAND,
Esquire.
AUGUST, 1885.

Town clerk
George Edward Sharland

This stylistic illuminated address comes in two sections.

The first section is an illuminated address, part printed (the borders), part designed and painted by hand. It was presented in 1885 by the Borough of Gravesend – when the mayor was Thomas Francis Wood – to George Edward Sharland for his forty years of service as Gravesend Town Clerk. He was also presented with his portrait, painted by J. Haynes Williams.

The second section is another illuminated address eight years later, in 1891, when Sharland retired, signed by George M. Arnold, the then current Mayor. Sharland lived at The Laurels, Milton, Gravesend and was aged sixty-six in 1885. He died in 1900 at the age of eighty-one.

Milton is on the east side of Gravesend, by the Thames estuary, not far from St George's Church where the memorial to Pocahontas is to be found. To understand why there is such a memorial to Pocahontas requires a back story.

Pocahontas was born in the late 1500s to a Chief of the Algonquian tribe, living in what is now Virginia. English settlers arrived in 1607 but were not welcome. When the ships sailed back to England, Captain John Smith and 104 other men were left to fend for themselves through the winter. The need for food brought the settlers into conflict with the Native Americans, Captain Smith was captured and, according to one story, was saved by a young Pocahontas on the point of being put to death.

Captain John Smith returned to England. The friction between settlers and Native Americans continued and Pocahontas was captured and held to ransom. She was taught the Christian faith, baptised as Rebecca

Page 1 of the address to George Edward Sharland given in 1885, illuminated by Waterlow Bros & Leyton, London.

The monogram on the cover of the address.

and met John Rolfe, a widower settler. Pocahontas and Rolfe married and had a son, Thomas, and the family of three sailed to England in 1616.

Captain Smith visited the family but was not welcomed by Pocahontas, for breaking promises he had made to her father.

She fell ill and the family chose to sail back to America in the spring of 1617. Pocahontas's health declined severely and

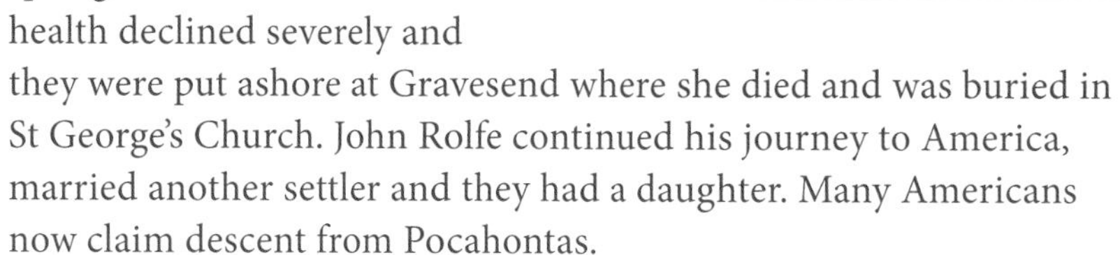

they were put ashore at Gravesend where she died and was buried in St George's Church. John Rolfe continued his journey to America, married another settler and they had a daughter. Many Americans now claim descent from Pocahontas.

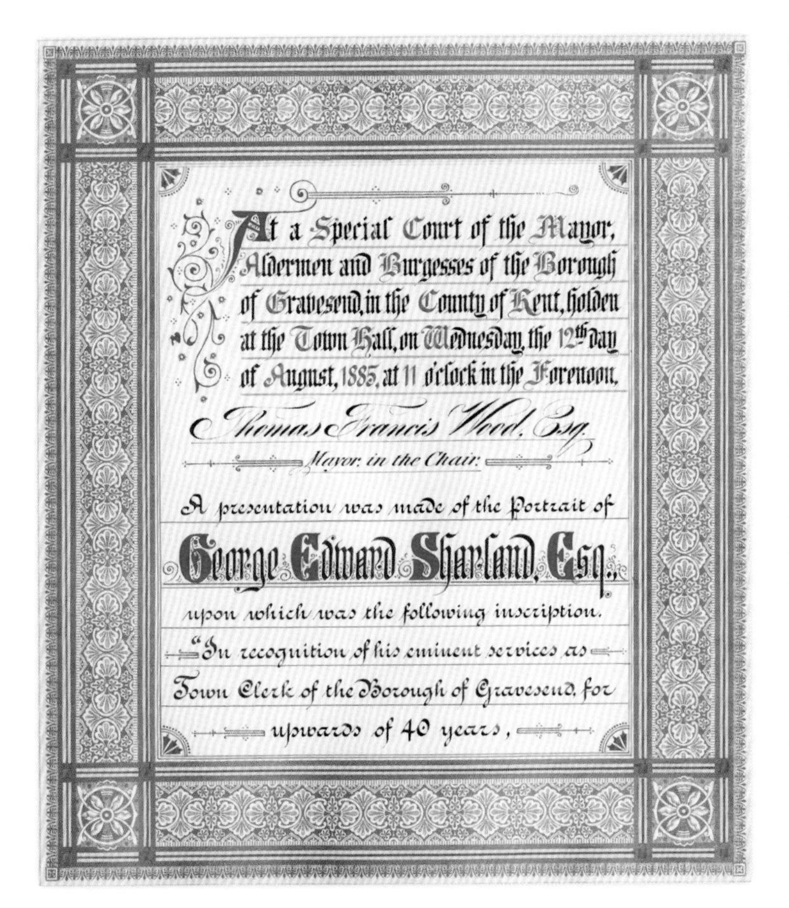

At a Special Court of the Mayor, Aldermen and Burgesses of the Borough of Gravesend, in the County of Kent, holden at the Town Hall, on Wednesday, the 12th day of August, 1885, at 11 o'clock in the Forenoon.

Thomas Francis Wood, Esq.

Mayor: in the Chair:

A presentation was made of the Portrait of

George Edward Sharland, Esq.,

upon which was the following inscription.

"In recognition of his eminent services as Town Clerk of the Borough of Gravesend, for upwards of 40 years,

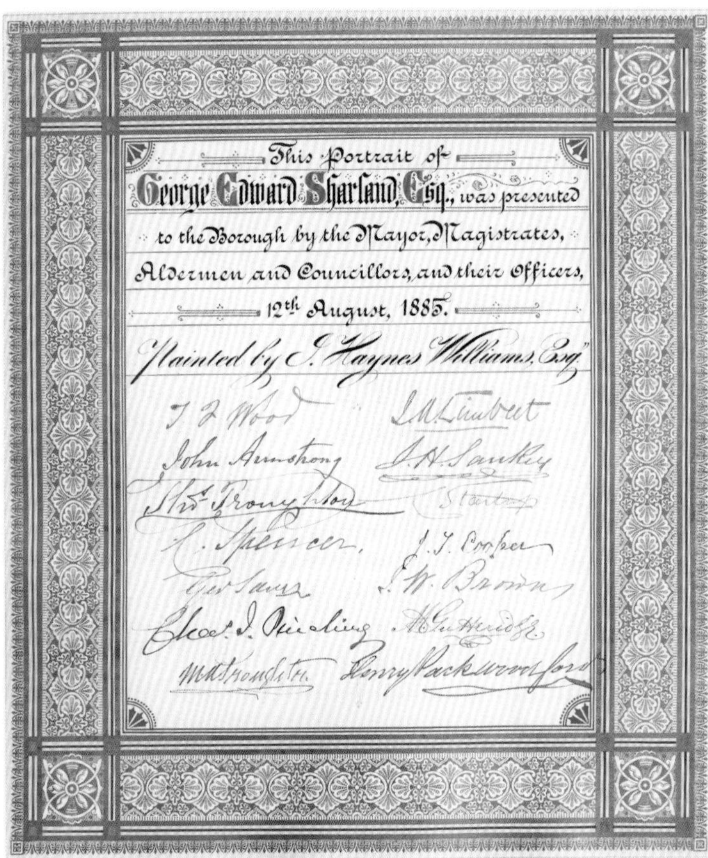

This Portrait of

George Edward Sharland, Esq., was presented to the Borough by the Mayor, Magistrates, Aldermen and Councillors, and their Officers, 12th August, 1885.

Painted by J. Haynes Williams, Esq."

Pages 2 and 3 of the address to
George Edward Sharland given in 1885.

A testimonial
John Death

In 1876 John Death of Cambridge was presented with a silver three-branch epergne (an ornamental centrepiece for a dining table, typically used for holding fruit or flowers), two three-light candelabra and a testimonial providing the inscription words used on the candelabra.

The presentation was in gratitude for Death's two years as Mayor of Cambridge over the period 1873–5, although he was also Mayor again from 1880–82. His gifts were presented by the Master of St Peter's College, Reverend H.W. Cookson, DD. St Peter's College, known as Peterhouse, is the oldest college in Cambridge, having been founded in 1284. The illuminator was F.C. Gower of St Edwards Passage.

Death ran a livery stable in Cambridge and also sat on the Parish Council.

Death laid the foundation stone of the Corn Exchange, on the corner of Corn Exchange Street and Guildhall Street in 1874. It was opened in 1875, with the stone of the building being made from Cornish granite from the Cheesewring Quarry.

According to Cambridge City Council's records, a few days after the Corn Exchange was opened a promenade concert was given by the Coldstream Guards and a local choral society. A mistake made during the playing of the National Anthem led to trouble, including rioters attacking the Mayor's house. A trial resulted and the incident received national attention.

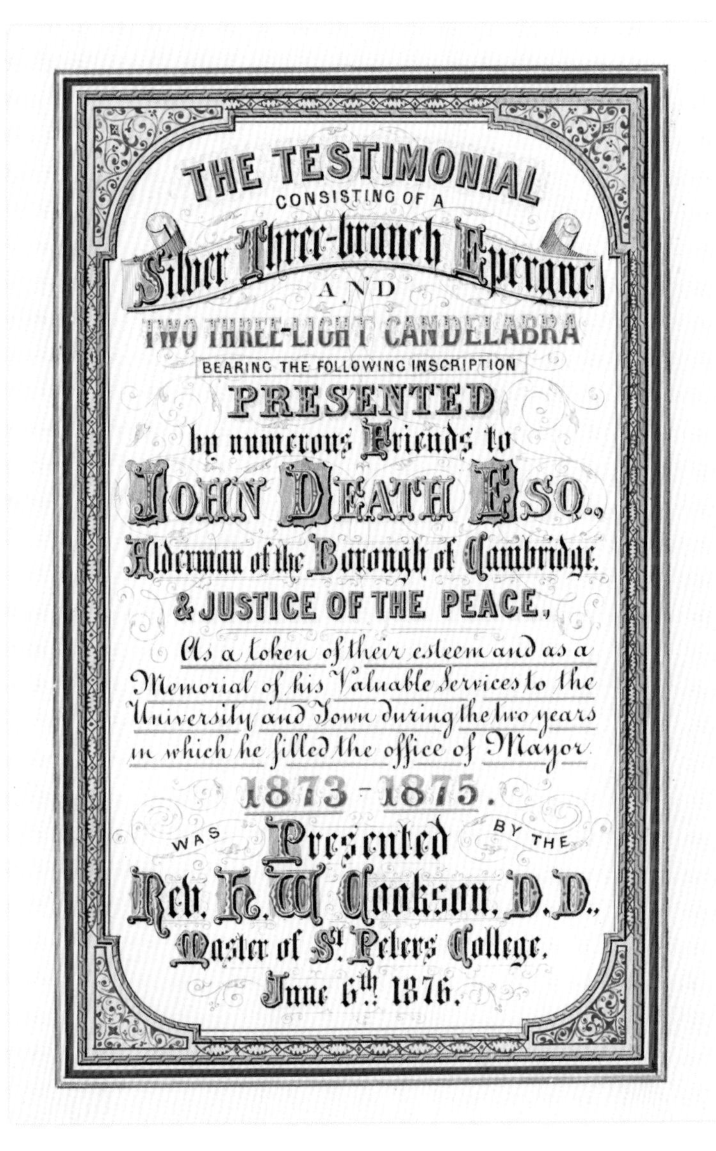

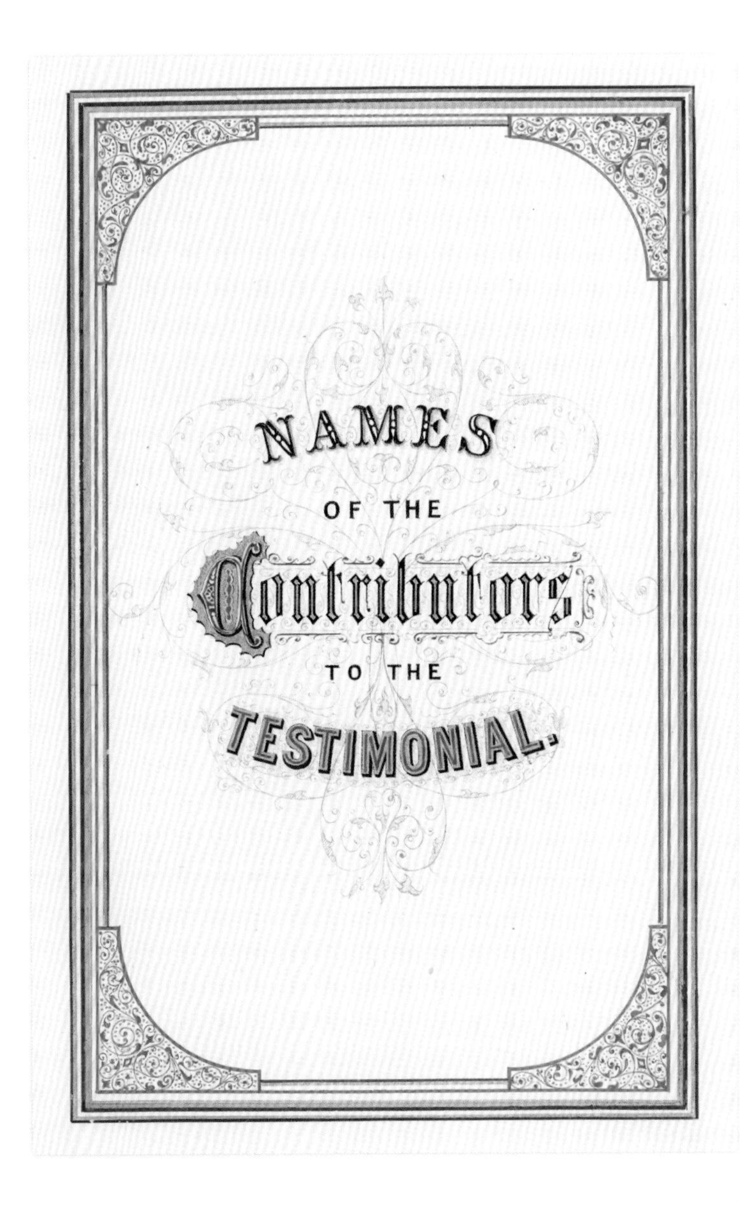

Three pages from the address to John Death given in 1876,
illuminated by F.C. Gower, St Edwards Passage, Cambridge.

To Sir Edward W. Fithian.

Address presented by the Association of Chambers of Commerce of the United Kingdom.

In conveying to you our hearty congratulations on the honour of Knighthood graciously conferred upon you by His Majesty, we desire to express our high appreciation of the valuable services which you have rendered to our Association for a period of nearly 40 years.

Pages 1 and 2 of the address to Sir Edward W. Fithian given in 1905, illuminated by Waterlow & Sons, London Wall.

'Monkey Town' resident
Sir Edward W. Fithian

Sir Edward W. Fithian was presented with a beautiful boxed illumination, together with 'a piece of plate and purse' in 1905, in honour of his knighthood and in gratitude for his forty years of service to the Association of Chambers of Commerce of the United Kingdom.

Sir Edward was the son of a bookseller, born in Heywood (known as 'Monkey Town'), in 1845. He went to Manchester Grammar School and King's College, London and became a barrister. He took a leading role in supporting commerce. In 1903 he was awarded Officier de

During that time the Membership of the Association has increased from 33 Chambers to 108. This gratifying result is due largely to your industry as its Secretary combined as it has been with unfailing tact and courtesy in the discharge of your varied and arduous duties. We therefore have pleasure in asking you to accept the Piece of Plate and Purse which accompany this Address and cordially wish you many years of health and happiness.

W. H. Holland President.

T. Craig-Brown Vice-Presidents.

Hon. Secretaries.

Instruction Publique by President Loubet of France for his services to the promotion of friendly relations between the UK and France.

The naming of Heywood as Monkey Town has an uncertain derivation. It may be based on Heal Bridge being called 'Ape' Bridge due to the derogatory name given to the builders. In the 1840s the Lancashire and Yorkshire Railway was being extended by Irish navvies. Around that time, apes were new to the UK with the first, Tommy, a chimpanzee, arriving at London Zoo in 1835, soon followed by Jenny, an orangutan.

Lord Mayor of London
Sir Rupert De la Bère of Crowborough

I have wondered if Sir Rupert De la Bère's name influenced the naming of Rupert Bear! The name Bère is likely to derive from either fort (ber), swine pasture (baer) or barley (bere), arising in southwest England.

Alderman Sir Rupert was the son of Reginald De la Bère in Addlestone. He went to Tonbridge School, served in the RAF during the First World War and served as a Member of Parliament for Evesham for fifteen years from 1935. He was a director of Hay's Wharf and was a City of London alderman, sheriff and then Mayor.

He was knighted in 1952, and made a baronet and Knight Commander of the Royal Victorian Order in 1953. I assume he chose to be 'of Crowborough' as he lived in the hill-top town in East Sussex, close to the Ashdown Forest, home of Winnie the Pooh and friends.

Sir Rupert was presented with an attractive illuminated scroll in celebration of being elected Lord Mayor of London in 1952. He was also a Knight of the Order of St John of Jerusalem, a Knight of the Order of the Polar Star in Sweden and a Knight of the Order of Dannebrog in Denmark.

He married Marguerite Humphrey, daughter of Lt Col Sir John Humphrey of Walton Leigh, Addlestone, in 1919. Sir Rupert and Marguerite had five children between 1920 and 1939.

The address to Sir Rupert De la Bère given in 1952, illuminated by Norris, 26 King Street, London.

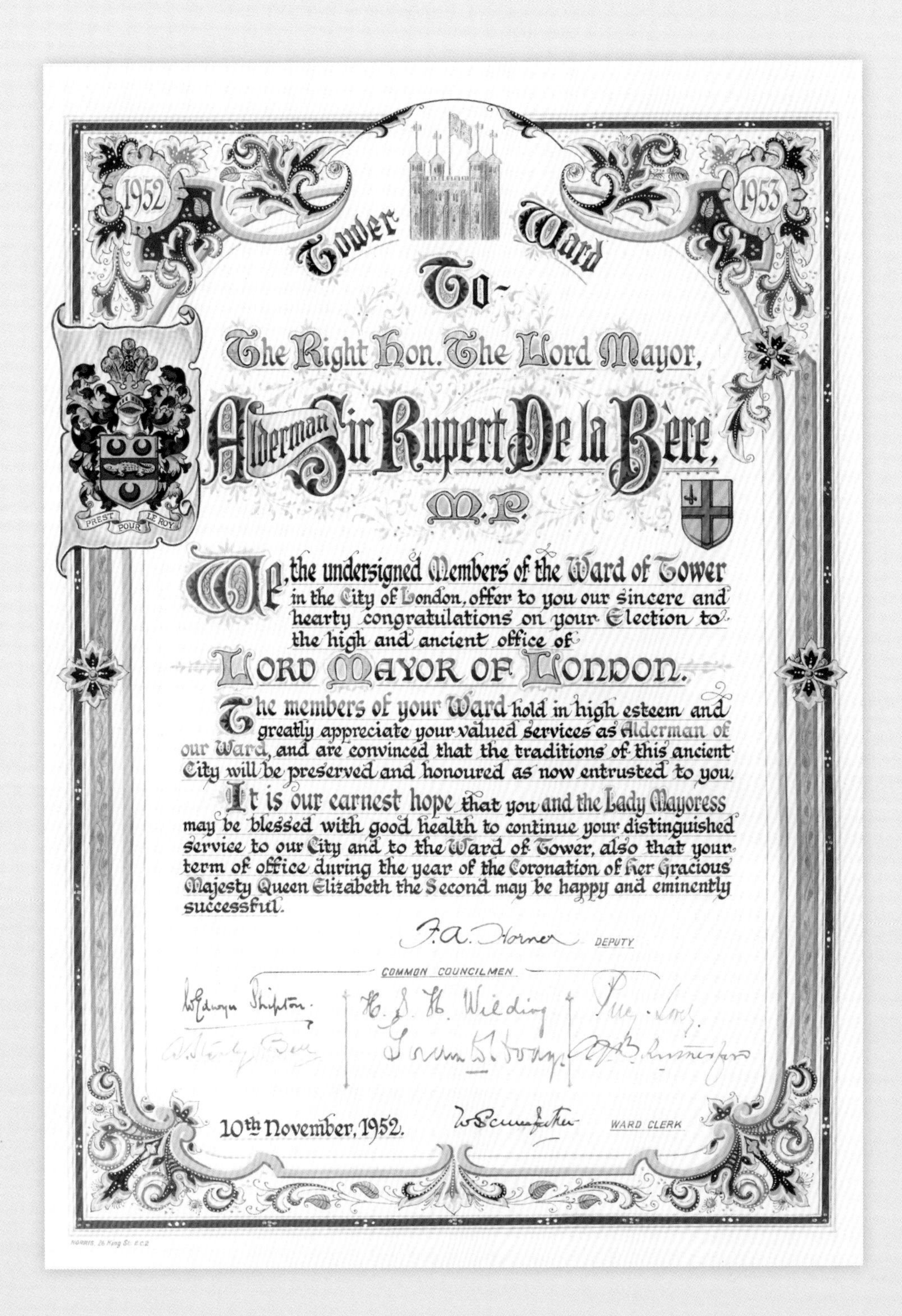

1952 1953

Tower Ward

To–

The Right Hon. The Lord Mayor,

Alderman Sir Rupert De la Bère,

M.P.

PREST POUR LE ROY

We, the undersigned Members of the Ward of Tower in the City of London, offer to you our sincere and hearty congratulations on your Election to the high and ancient office of

LORD MAYOR OF LONDON.

The members of your Ward hold in high esteem and greatly appreciate your valued services as Alderman of our Ward, and are convinced that the traditions of this ancient City will be preserved and honoured as now entrusted to you.

It is our earnest hope that you and the Lady Mayoress may be blessed with good health to continue your distinguished service to our City and to the Ward of Tower, also that your term of office during the year of the Coronation of her Gracious Majesty Queen Elizabeth the Second may be happy and eminently successful.

F.A. Horner DEPUTY

COMMON COUNCILMEN

10th November, 1952.

WARD CLERK

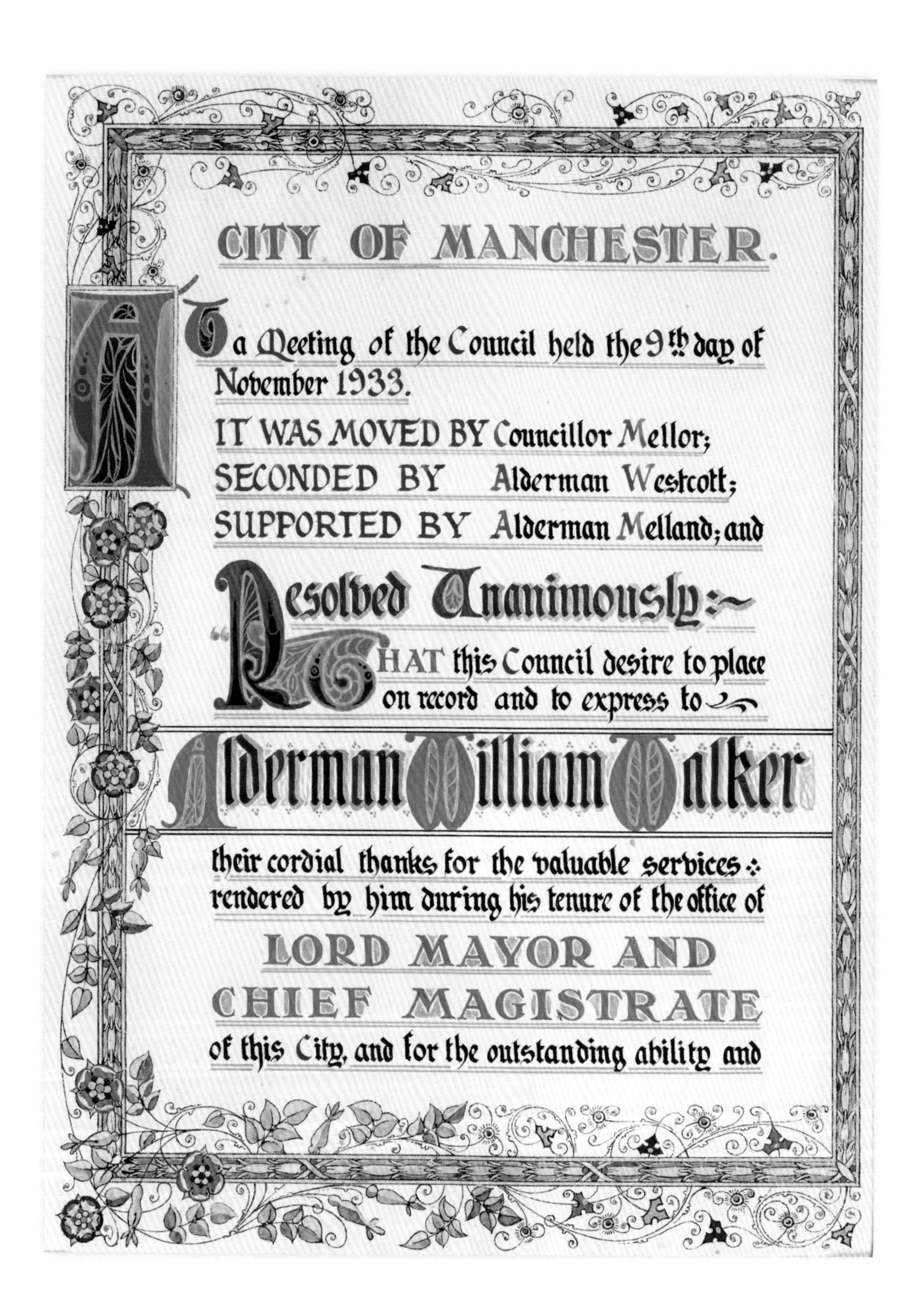

CITY OF MANCHESTER.

At a Meeting of the Council held the 9th day of November 1933.

IT WAS MOVED BY Councillor Mellor;
SECONDED BY Alderman Westcott;
SUPPORTED BY Alderman Melland; and

Resolved Unanimously:–

"THAT this Council desire to place on record and to express to

Alderman William Walker

their cordial thanks for the valuable services rendered by him during his tenure of the office of

LORD MAYOR AND CHIEF MAGISTRATE

of this City, and for the outstanding ability and

Lord Mayor of Manchester
Alderman Sir William Walker, JP, LLD

Two stunning illuminated addresses were given to Alderman Sir William Walker in 1933 and 1959.

In 1933 Alderman Walker was thanked for his service as Lord Mayor of Manchester and Chief Magistrate over the period 1932–3. Also, thanks were given to Lady Mayoress Mrs Davidson Peattie. I have not found why the Mayor and Mayoress had different names!

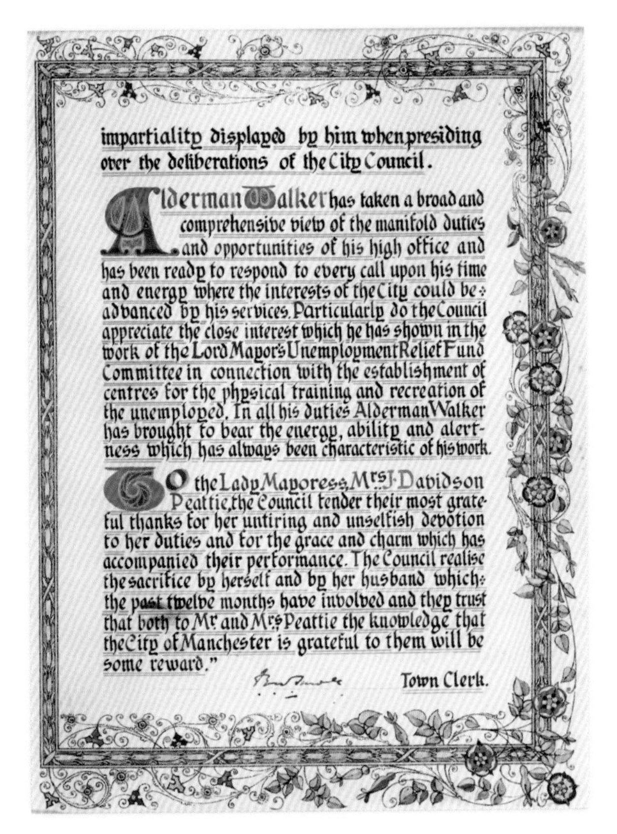
impartiality displayed by him when presiding over the deliberations of the City Council.

Alderman Walker has taken a broad and comprehensive view of the manifold duties and opportunities of his high office and has been ready to respond to every call upon his time and energy where the interests of the City could be advanced by his services. Particularly do the Council appreciate the close interest which he has shown in the work of the Lord Mayor's Unemployment Relief Fund Committee in connection with the establishment of centres for the physical training and recreation of the unemployed. In all his duties Alderman Walker has brought to bear the energy, ability and alertness which has always been characteristic of his work.

To the Lady Mayoress, Mrs J. Davidson Peattie, the Council tender their most grateful thanks for her untiring and unselfish devotion to her duties and for the grace and charm which has accompanied their performance. The Council realise the sacrifice by herself and by her husband which the past twelve months have involved and they trust that both to Mr and Mrs Peattie the knowledge that the City of Manchester is grateful to them will be some reward."

Town Clerk.

Pages 1 and 2 of the address to Alderman Sir William Walker given in 1933.

By 1959 Walker had become Sir William Walker, JP, LLD and had served fifty years on the City Council.

He worked in the electricity industry as a director of Henry Simon Ltd, which made machinery for the granary and coal industries. The company was founded by Henry Gustav Simon, a Polish immigrant, who made and sold rolling machines for grinding grain. He supplied the first automated rolling machines to McDougall Brothers who milled flour. Machines were sold worldwide, including equipment in the Far East for rice milling. The business evolved by takeover and merger and was subsequently sold to the Japanese firm, Satake Group.

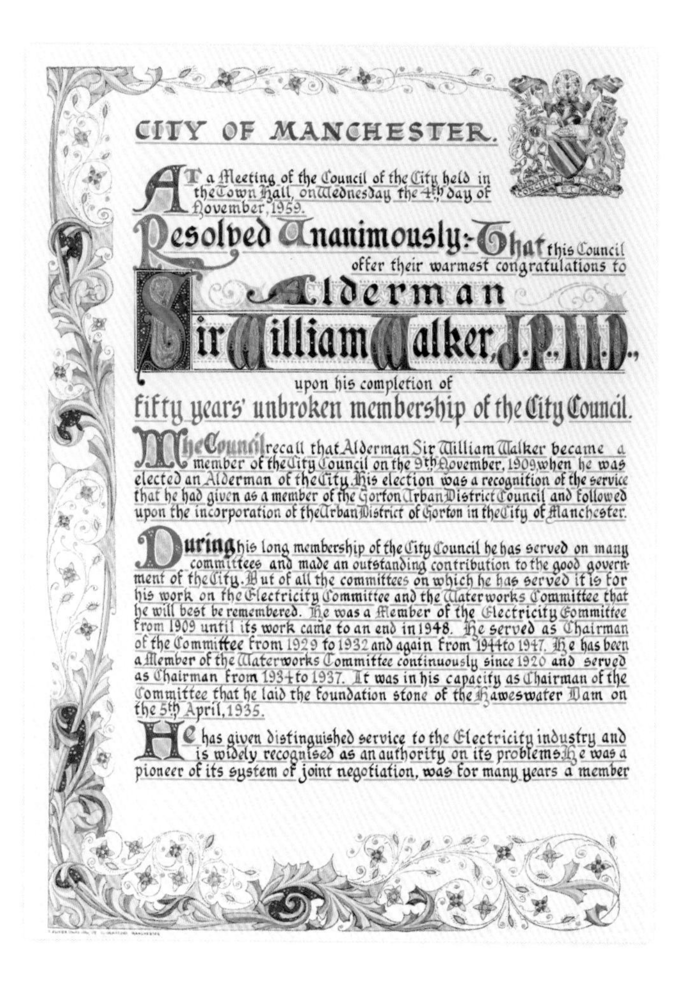

CITY OF MANCHESTER.

AT a Meeting of the Council of the City held in the Town Hall, on Wednesday the 4th day of November, 1959.

Resolved Unanimously:- That this Council offer their warmest congratulations to

Alderman

Sir William Walker, J.P., LL.D.,

upon his completion of

fifty years' unbroken membership of the City Council.

The Council recall that Alderman Sir William Walker became a member of the City Council on the 9th November, 1909, when he was elected an Alderman of the City. His election was a recognition of the service that he had given as a member of the Gorton Urban District Council and followed upon the incorporation of the Urban District of Gorton in the City of Manchester.

During his long membership of the City Council he has served on many committees and made an outstanding contribution to the good government of the City. But of all the committees on which he has served it is for his work on the Electricity Committee and the Waterworks Committee that he will best be remembered. He was a Member of the Electricity Committee from 1909 until its work came to an end in 1948. He served as Chairman of the Committee from 1929 to 1932 and again from 1944 to 1947. He has been a Member of the Waterworks Committee continuously since 1920 and served as Chairman from 1934 to 1937. It was in his capacity as Chairman of the Committee that he laid the foundation stone of the Haweswater Dam on the 5th April, 1935.

He has given distinguished service to the Electricity industry and is widely recognised as an authority on its problems. He was a pioneer of its system of joint negotiation, was for many years a member

Pages 1 and 2 of the address to Alderman Sir William Walker, JP, LLD given in 1959.

Sir William joined the Manchester City Council in 1909 and particularly supported Manchester's water and electricity supplies. He helped in the acquisition of machinery for the electrical power industry, and laid the Foundation Stone for the Haweswater Dam in Cumbria.

He joined the Central Electricity Board in 1926 and was President of the Incorporated Municipal Electrical Association. He was made a Knight Bachelor in 1945 and awarded an honorary Doctor of Law from the University of Manchester in 1952.

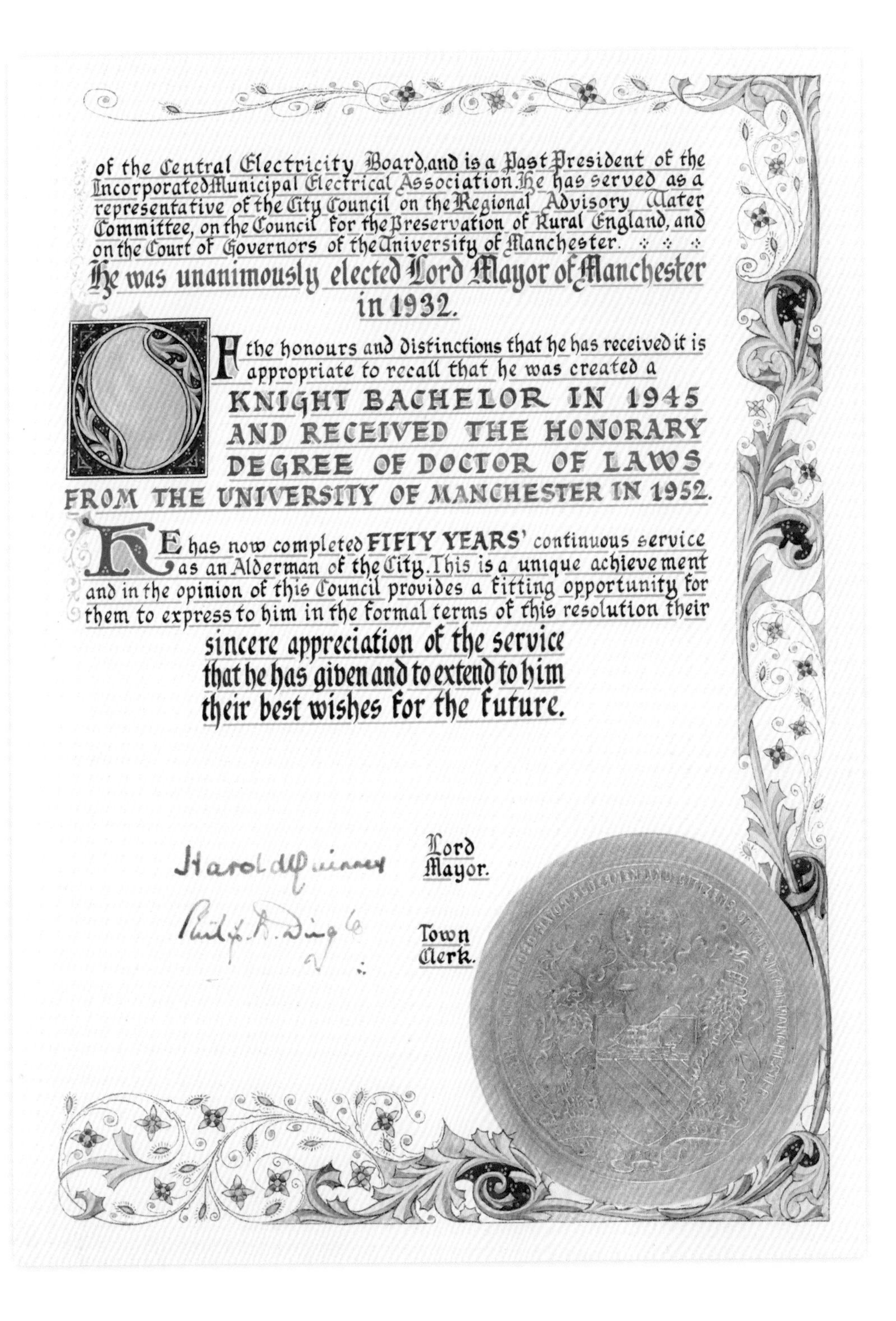
of the Central Electricity Board, and is a Past President of the Incorporated Municipal Electrical Association. He has served as a representative of the City Council on the Regional Advisory Water Committee, on the Council for the Preservation of Rural England, and on the Court of Governors of the University of Manchester.

He was unanimously elected Lord Mayor of Manchester in 1932.

Of the honours and distinctions that he has received it is appropriate to recall that he was created a KNIGHT BACHELOR IN 1945 AND RECEIVED THE HONORARY DEGREE OF DOCTOR OF LAWS FROM THE UNIVERSITY OF MANCHESTER IN 1952.

He has now completed FIFTY YEARS' continuous service as an Alderman of the City. This is a unique achievement and in the opinion of this Council provides a fitting opportunity for them to express to him in the formal terms of this resolution their sincere appreciation of the service that he has given and to extend to him their best wishes for the future.

Lord Mayor.

Town Clerk.

CLUBS AND SOCIETIES

The Weir '25' Stag Club
Andrew Alexander Morton Weir, Lord Inverforth

This is a simple but sweet illuminated address in a folder with the presentation on one side and signatures on the other. Lord Inverforth is being thanked by the Weir '25' Stag Club for an inaugural dinner at the Trocadero in 1957. The few words are nicely written, neat and colourful, with a fine watercolour painting of a stag.

Like many illuminated addresses, it is not immediately obvious what the organisation is that is presenting its gratitude and at which Trocadero the event took place in. Therefore, the details that follow are based on supposition.

The 1st Baron Lord Inverforth was Andrew Weir, President of Andrew Weir Shipping and Trading Co. Ltd – ship owners and merchants. *Burke's Peerage* states he was born in 1865, given his peerage in 1919 and died in 1955. He lived at The Hill, North End, Hampstead Heath, later known as Inverforth House, which he bought from the estate of William Lever, 1st Viscount Leverhulme, who established Lever Brothers, the manufacturer of Sunlight Soap, Lux and Life Buoy.

The first baron's eldest son, Andrew Alexander Morton Weir (1897–1975), became the 2nd Baron Inverforth on the death of his father in 1955. Therefore, it would appear that the 1957 illumination was given to the 2nd Baron, the Chairman of the Andrew Weir Shipping and Trading Co. Ltd. Both sons of the 2nd Baron also joined the business.

The company owned passenger ships, cargo ships and oil tankers. The first sailing ship had been bought in 1885 and the first steam ship in Glasgow in 1896. Soon after, the company's ships were registered and known under the name Bank Line. In 2014 it went into voluntary administration.

The address to Lord Inverforth given in 1957.

It is not clear what the Weir '25' Stag Club was. A guess would be that it was an association of the company's employees who had served for more than twenty-five years. The club appears to have begun in 1957, launched with a meal at the Trocadero in Coventry Street, London, which in 1957 was a restaurant. It was built in 1896 as a J. Lyons & Co. restaurant. It is now an entertainment centre.

Mason
W. Bro. A.C. Morton

Alpheus Cleophas Morton PM (Past Master) was a member of the Masonic Albion Lodge No. 9 and was honoured by his fellow members for reaching fifty years of membership from 1865 to 1915. He was presented with a bright illuminated address on 2 February 1915.

While Albion Lodge No. 9 had originally been formed in 1769, it was re-consecrated in 1889. In the same year it met at the Ship and Turtle public house in Leadenhall Street, London. It now meets at Freemasons' Hall, Great Queen Street.

The meeting to honour Morton was held at Restaurant Frascati on Oxford Street, famous for its luxury and cuisine. It had been established in the late 1890s at 32 Oxford Street. It had gold leaf decoration on the outside and a Winter Garden inside below a large glass dome. It was well known for its use of flower decorations and had a ballroom for dancing to a resident orchestra. Unfortunately, it was destroyed in the Second World War.

Alpheus Cleophas Morton had an intriguing name, although it is not clear why he was given it. He was born in 1840 and educated in Canada. He became an architect, lived in Clapham and joined the City of London Corporation in 1882. He was responsible for the opening of

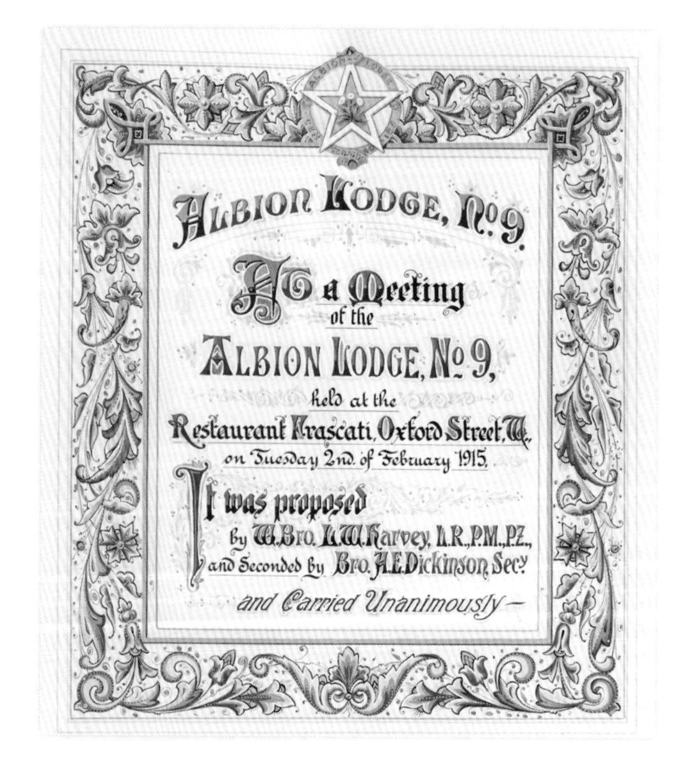
Albion Lodge, No. 9

At a Meeting of the Albion Lodge, No. 9, held at the Restaurant Frascati, Oxford Street, W., on Tuesday 2nd. of February 1915,

It was proposed by W. Bro. L.W. Harvey, L.R., P.M., P.Z., and Seconded by Bro. A.E. Dickinson, Secy and Carried Unanimously –

Page 1 and 2 of the address to W. Bro. A.C. Morton given in 1915.

"That the hearty congratulations of the Lodge be given to

W. Bro. Alpheus Cleophas Morton,

P.M.,

on the occasion of the Jubilee of his Membership. He having been initiated in this Lodge on the 7th of March, 1865."

It was also Moved and Carried Unanimously

"That the above Resolution be engrossed on Vellum and presented to W. Bro. Morton."

[illegible] W.M.

J. D. R. Lewis S.W.

[illegible] J.W.

the park in Finsbury Circus and established the practice of presenting mulberries from the park to the Lord Mayor of London. Morton also saved St Dunstan-in-the-West on Fleet Street and a number of other London churches that were proposed for demolition in 1919. He was a churchwarden of St Dunstan-in-the-West.

Morton was MP for Peterborough from 1886–95 and for Sutherland from 1906–18, was knighted in 1918 and died in 1923.

Lord Mayor of Leeds
The Rt Hon. Lord Airedale of Gledhow

Lord Airedale was honoured by the High Court of the Ancient Order of Foresters in 1907. He was presented with a boxed, neat illuminated address. However, the words do not make clear what the honour was for, and the gothic words are not easy to read! It says:

... for the fraternal sympathy and hospitality extended to the representatives of the Order on the occasion of the annual meeting being held in Leeds, and, in commemoration of the fact that his honoured father was High Chief Ranger of the Order.

Perhaps he paid for the refreshments!

Gledhow sounds to me as if it should be a hamlet in the Scottish Highlands but it is, in fact, a suburb to the northeast of Leeds. Airedale is an area in Yorkshire, with the River Aire – which is more than 90 miles long – travelling through Leeds.

Within the illuminated address are two small photographs, one of the Albert Hall in Leeds and the other of Gledhow Hall. The Albert Hall began as the Mechanical Institution and Literary Society, and is now the City Museum.

Gledhow Hall was the family home of Sir James Kitson who

became 1st Baron Airedale in 1907. He was the first Lord Mayor of Leeds in 1895. Previously, Leeds had only had mayors, and much earlier an alderman, as the head of the Borough Committee. Gledhow Hall had been built in 1766 by the same architect who had designed Harewood House. The 1st Baron Airedale had made his money from iron and steel, and from making train engines.

The son of the 1st Baron Airedale, Albert Kitson, inherited Gledhow Hall in 1911 when his father died, and it was used as a hospital in the First World War by the St John's Ambulance Voluntary Aid Detachment.

Albert had married Florence Schunck in 1890, the daughter of Edward von Schunck who had married Kate Lupton, whose family were well known landowners around Leeds. Edward owned the neighbouring Gledhow Wood Estate, Kate had lived at Potternewton Hall and her father, Darnton Lupton had been a Mayor of Leeds. Kate's cousin, Francis Martineau Lupton lived close by on the Newton Park Estate, whose eldest daughter Olive married Richard Noel Middleton, a solicitor. Olive and Richard are the great-grandparents of Kate Middleton, now the Duchess of Cambridge.

Olive lived at Gledhow Hall in the First World War with her second cousin, Lady Airedale, and served as a nurse with the St John's Ambulance Voluntary Aid Detachment.

The illuminated presentation to Lord Airedale was given by The Ancient Order of Foresters, a society formed in Rochdale in 1834. It was based on a reformation of the Royal Foresters Society. It is not the

Independent Order of Foresters which was created in 1874 when the North American Foresters broke away; the UK part of the Independent Order is called Forester Life.

The Ancient Order of Foresters has local branches called courts, named after the law courts of the royal forests. It is a Friendly Society offering member benefits such as discretionary grants and charitable donations.

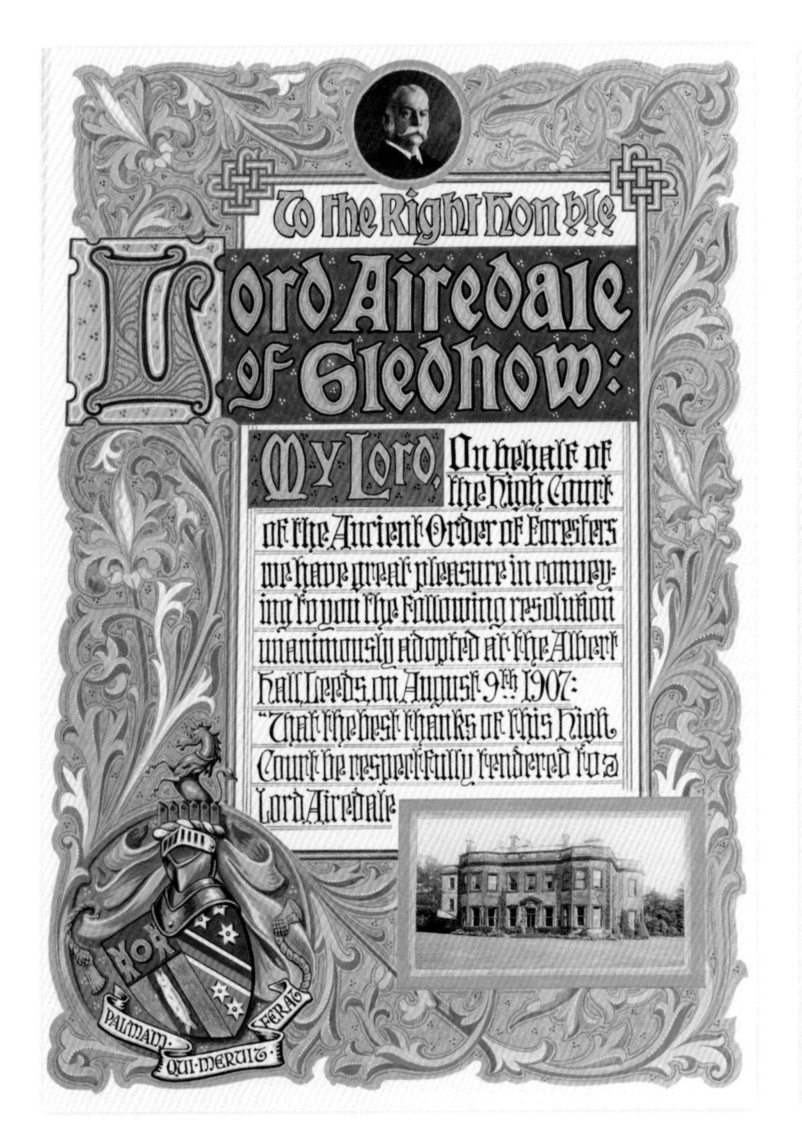

To the Right Hon.ble

Lord Airedale of Gledhow:

My Lord, On behalf of the High Court of the Ancient Order of Foresters we have great pleasure in conveying to you the following resolution unanimously adopted at the Albert Hall, Leeds, on August 9th 1907:

"That the best thanks of this High Court be respectfully tendered to Lord Airedale

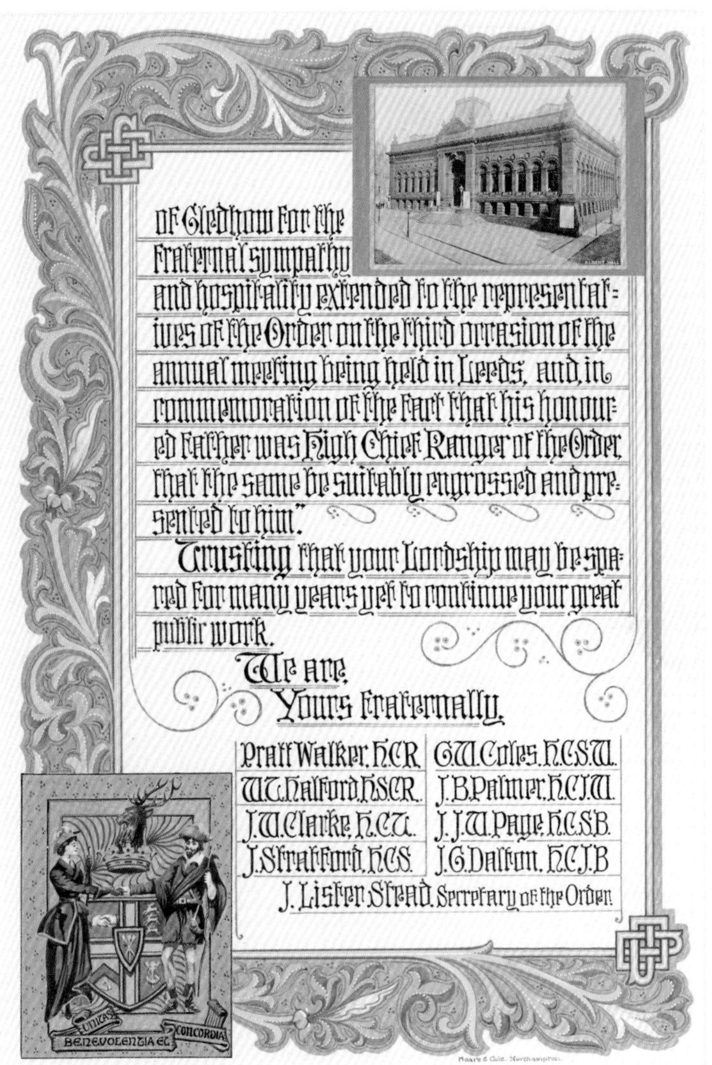

of Gledhow for the fraternal sympathy and hospitality extended to the representatives of the Order on the third occasion of the annual meeting being held in Leeds, and in commemoration of the fact that his honoured father was High Chief Ranger of the Order that the same be suitably engrossed and presented to him."

Trusting that your Lordship may be spared for many years yet to continue your great public work.

We are,
Yours fraternally,

Pratt Walker. H.C.R.	G.W. Coles. H.C.S.W.
W.C. Halford. H.S.C.R.	J.B. Palmer. H.C.J.W.
J.W. Clarke. H.C.T.	J.J.W. Page. H.C.S.B.
J. Stratford. H.C.S.	J.G. Dalton. H.C.J.B.

J. Lister Stead. Secretary of the Order.

Pages 1 and 2 of the address to Rt Hon. Lord Airedale of Gledhow given in 1907, illuminated by Hoare & Cole, Northampton.

Baronet
Lt-Gen. Sir Frederick Wellington John Fitzwygram, Bt

Many historically important families built their fame and fortune in the military or in business. One of these families, the Fitzwygrams, were involved in both.

Lt-Gen. Sir Frederick Wellington John Fitzwygram, Bt became the 4th Baronet in 1873. He was a cavalry officer with the 6th Inniskilling Dragoons, serving in the Crimean War and later in Aldershot.

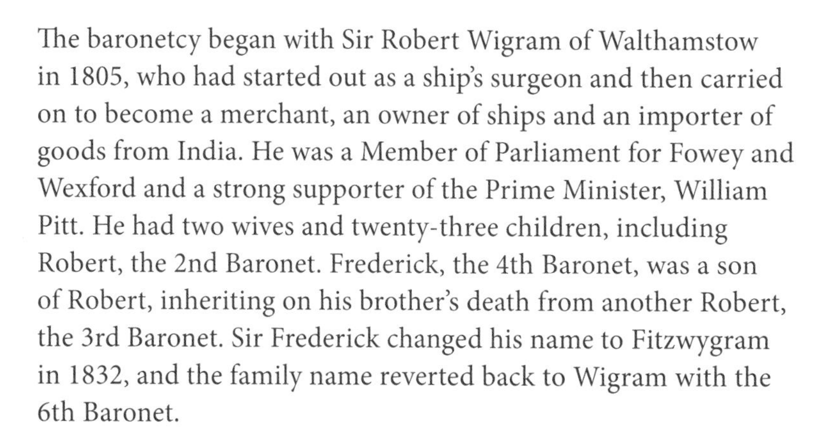

The baronetcy began with Sir Robert Wigram of Walthamstow in 1805, who had started out as a ship's surgeon and then carried on to become a merchant, an owner of ships and an importer of goods from India. He was a Member of Parliament for Fowey and Wexford and a strong supporter of the Prime Minister, William Pitt. He had two wives and twenty-three children, including Robert, the 2nd Baronet. Frederick, the 4th Baronet, was a son of Robert, inheriting on his brother's death from another Robert, the 3rd Baronet. Sir Frederick changed his name to Fitzwygram in 1832, and the family name reverted back to Wigram with the 6th Baronet.

Historically, 'Fitz' meant 'son of', but sometimes it was used to denote illegitimacy.

Sir Frederick bought Leigh Park in 1875, an estate close to Portsmouth that had originally been a farm but was converted into an estate by Sir George Staunton. The estate passed to his descendants and was bought by the city of Portsmouth in 1944. The house was demolished in 1959, except for the Gothic Library

The address to Lt-Gen. Sir Frederick Fitzwygram, Bt given in 1895, illuminated by Waterlow & Sons Ltd, London.

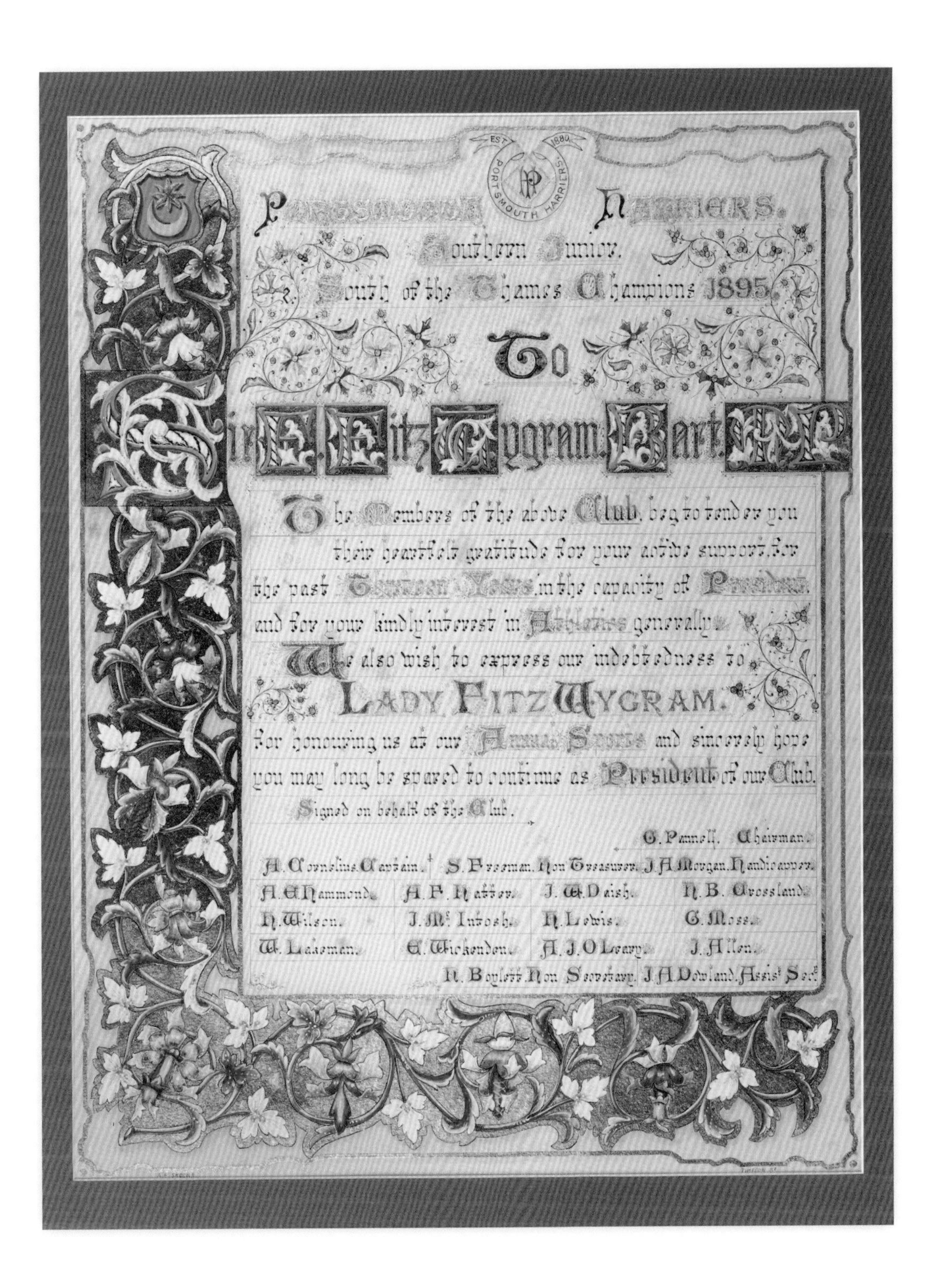

EST 1880 PORTSMOUTH HARRIERS

Portsmouth Harriers.
Southern Junior.
South of the Thames Champions 1895.

To

Sir F. Fitz Wygram. Bart. M.P.

The Members of the above Club, beg to tender you their heartfelt gratitude for your active support, for the past Thirteen Years, in the capacity of President, and for your kindly interest in Athletics generally.

We also wish to express our indebtedness to

LADY FITZ WYGRAM.

for honouring us at our Annual Sports and sincerely hope you may long be spared to continue as President of our Club.

Signed on behalf of the Club.

G. Pannell. Chairman.

A. Cornelius. Captain.	S. Freeman. Hon Treasurer.	J. A. Morgan. Handicapper.

A. C. Hammond.	A. F. Hatter.	J. W. Daish.	H. B. Crossland.
H. Wilson.	J. Mc Intosh.	H. Lewis.	G. Moss.
W. Lakeman.	E. Wickenden.	A. J. O Leary.	J. Allen.

H. Boylett Hon Secretary. J. A. Dowland. Assis^t Sec^y

(which still exists today), and the estate was converted to one of the largest council housing estates in the country, built for the post-Second World War homeless of Portsmouth and a park, now Staunton Country Park.

Sir Frederick was very involved in public life, especially around Portsmouth, and frequently opened his grounds and gardens to the public. He was a member of the Royal College of Veterinary Surgeons and the author of *Horses and Stables*, published in 1869, which concentrated on the care of horses.

The first illuminated address, a striking picture, finely embellished in gold, was given in 1895 by the Portsmouth Harrier Athletics Club of which Sir Frederick was its president. Like many paper- and card-based items from the past, the background picture colour has turned brown. It would originally have been white.

In 1900 Sir Frederick retired as a Member of Parliament, and the constituents in the Southern Division of Hampshire presented him with a neat, colourful illuminated address in gratitude for his sixteen years of service from 1884.

The address to Lt-Gen. Sir Frederick Fitzwygram, Bt given in 1900, illuminated by A.F. Skerns, Timpson Road, Portsmouth.

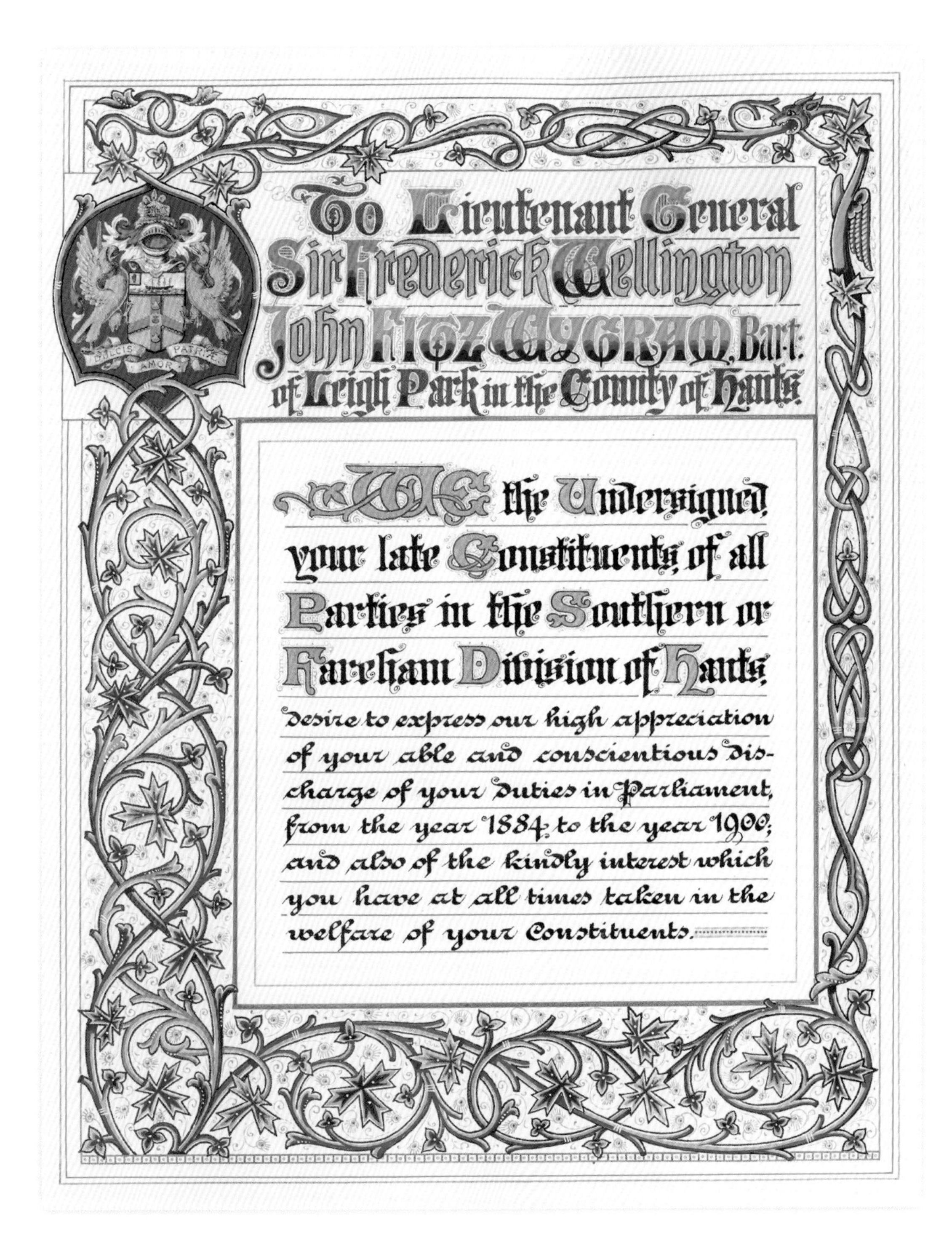

DULCIS AMOR PATRIAE

To Lieutenant General Sir Frederick Wellington John FitzWygram, Bart. of Leigh Park in the County of Hants.

We the Undersigned your late Constituents, of all Parties in the Southern or Fareham Division of Hants;

desire to express our high appreciation of your able and conscientious discharge of your duties in Parliament, from the year 1884, to the year 1900; and also of the kindly interest which you have at all times taken in the welfare of your Constituents.

Father and son
Matthew Fox Harrison and Frank Fox Harrison

Both father (Matthew) and son (Frank) supported the Walsall Licensed Victuallers and Beer Retailers Friendly & Protection Society.

Matthew served a phenomenal fifty-six years as the Secretary and was given his beautiful illumination in 1946 at the age of eighty-seven. He had the designated initials 'FAI' after his name, being a Fellow of the Auctioneers and Estate Agents Institute of the UK. He ran the business of Fox & Harrison, Auctioneers and Valuers in Lower Hall Lane, Walsall, first getting his auctioneers' licence in 1887. His connection with the Licensed Victuallers was as a result of managing property in Walsall, including the tenants of licensed properties.

Monogram from the address to Frank Fox Harrison.

Frank joined his father's business and also took his father's role as Secretary of the Licensed Victuallers Society. His presentation was given in 1959, also by the Licensed Victuallers Society, in celebration of him being elected as the Mayor of Walsall. Frank became a councillor in 1942, Mayor in 1958 and an alderman in 1962.

Both illuminations were superbly illustrated by the Municipal School of Art and Crafts, later known as the Walsall College of Arts and Technology. Unusually, both illuminations provide the recipients' home addresses.

Top: Page 1 and 2 of the address to Matthew Harrison given in 1946, illuminated by the Municipal School of Arts and Crafts, Goodall Street, Walsall.

Bottom: Page 1 and 2 of the address to Frank Harrison given in 1959.

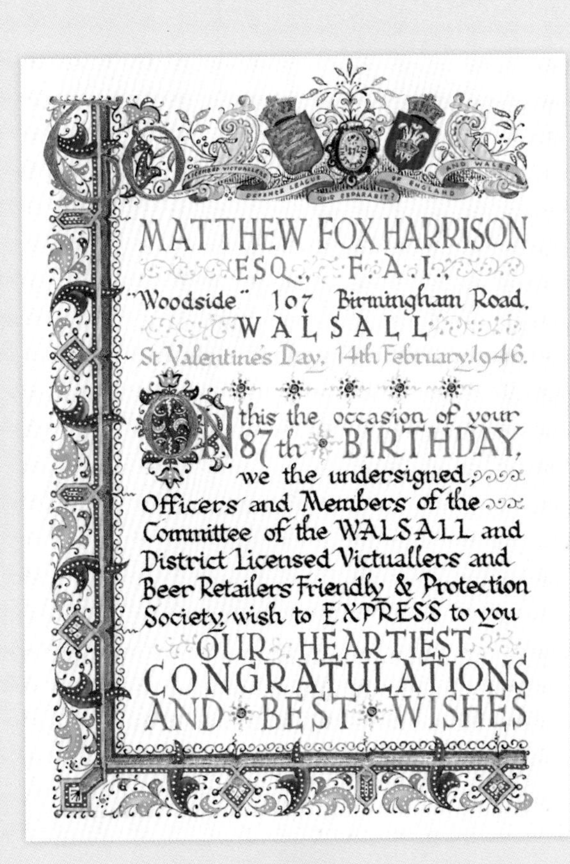

MATTHEW FOX HARRISON
ESQ., F.A.I.,
"Woodside" 107 Birmingham Road,
WALSALL
St. Valentine's Day, 14th February, 1946.

On this the occasion of your 87th BIRTHDAY, we the undersigned Officers and Members of the Committee of the WALSALL and District Licensed Victuallers and Beer Retailers Friendly & Protection Society wish to EXPRESS to you OUR HEARTIEST CONGRATULATIONS AND BEST WISHES

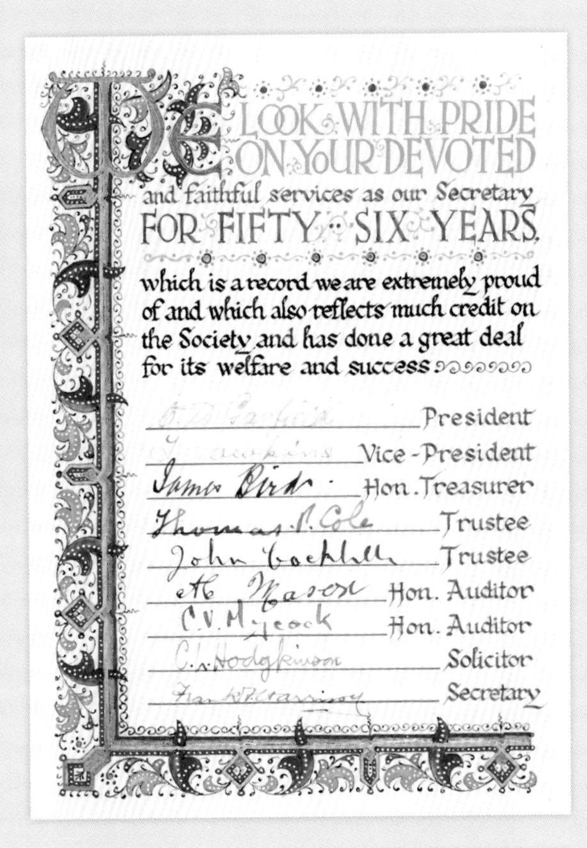

We LOOK WITH PRIDE ON YOUR DEVOTED and faithful services as our Secretary FOR FIFTY SIX YEARS which is a record we are extremely proud of and which also reflects much credit on the Society and has done a great deal for its welfare and success

President
Vice-President
James Bird Hon. Treasurer
Thomas P. Cole Trustee
John Cockhill Trustee
H. Mason Hon. Auditor
C.V. Mycock Hon. Auditor
C.L. Hodgkinson Solicitor
Secretary

His Worship the Mayor of Walsall · Councillor
FRANK
FOX·HARRISON
F.R.I.C.S., F.A.I.
Greenacre, Beacon Road, Walsall, Staffs.

The Officers and Members of the Walsall and District Licensed Victuallers & Beer Retailers Friendly and Protection Society desire to express to their Secretary

Their heartiest congratulations & good wishes on his election as Mayor of the Ancient County Borough of Walsall for the year 1958-59. Following the long and distinguished record of service of his late father, with whom he acted for many years as Assistant Secretary and succeeded as Secretary to the Society in 1946. We are very proud to acknowledge with sincere thanks and appreciation his generous devotion & kindly encouragement which have contributed so much to the welfare and success of the Society.

His numerous public activities & associations have gained the admiration & respect of the citizens of Walsall & his elevation to the office of the Chief Citizen of the Borough was most worthily deserved and highly justified. As a mark of their respect & appreciation the members present this small token of their esteem and sincerely trust that the Society may be honoured with his guidance & friendship for many years to come.

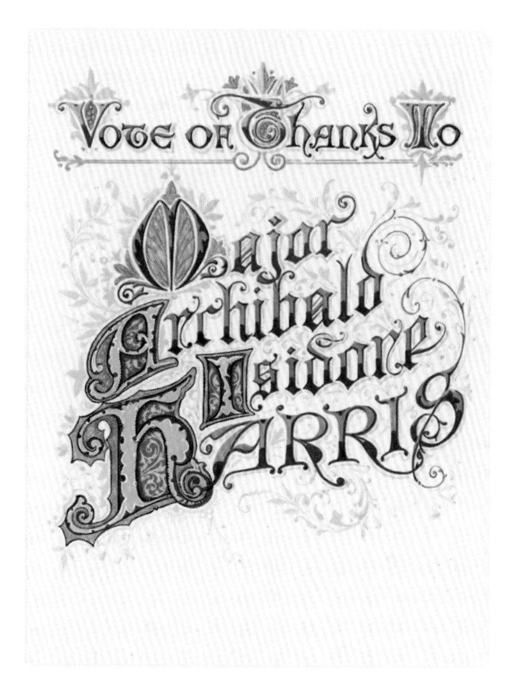

Pages 1, 2 and 3 of the address to Major Archibald Isidore Harris given in 1939.

Federation president
Major Archibald Isidore Harris

Major Archibald Isidore Harris was President of the Timber Trade Federation of the UK from 1937 and was thanked for his service with a neat book when his presidency ended in 1939.

The book includes the badge of University College School (UCS), oak leaves and the motto *Paulatim*. UCS is an independent school in Hampstead and counts Sir Roger Bannister, Sir Dirk Bogarde and Sir Chris Bonington amongst its past pupils. The school's motto *Paulitim Sed Fermiter* means 'Slowly but surely'.

Major Harris (later Sir Archibald Harris) was a major in France in the First World War and was twice mentioned in despatches. He worked in the timber trade all his life. After his presidency of the Federation he served as Timber Controller in the Ministry of Trade from 1939–47.

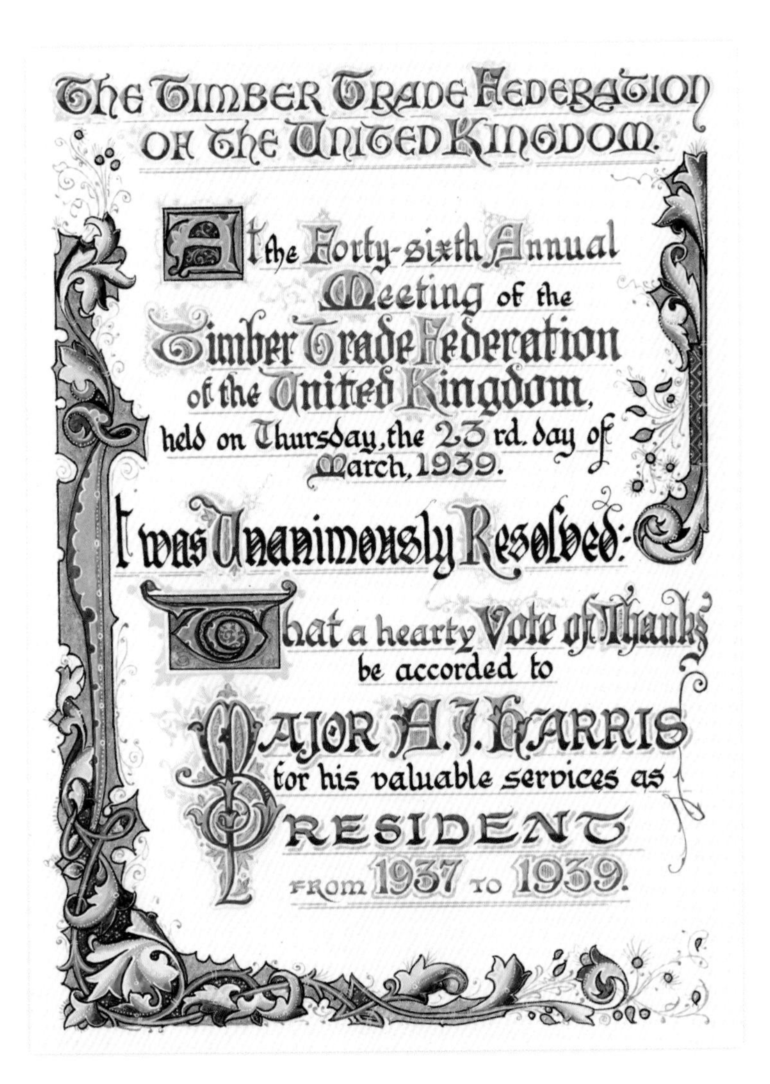

The Timber Trade Federation of the United Kingdom.

At the Forty-sixth Annual Meeting of the Timber Trade Federation of the United Kingdom, held on Thursday, the 23 rd. day of March, 1939.

It was Unanimously Resolved:

That a hearty Vote of Thanks be accorded to Major A. J. Harris for his valuable services as President from 1937 to 1939.

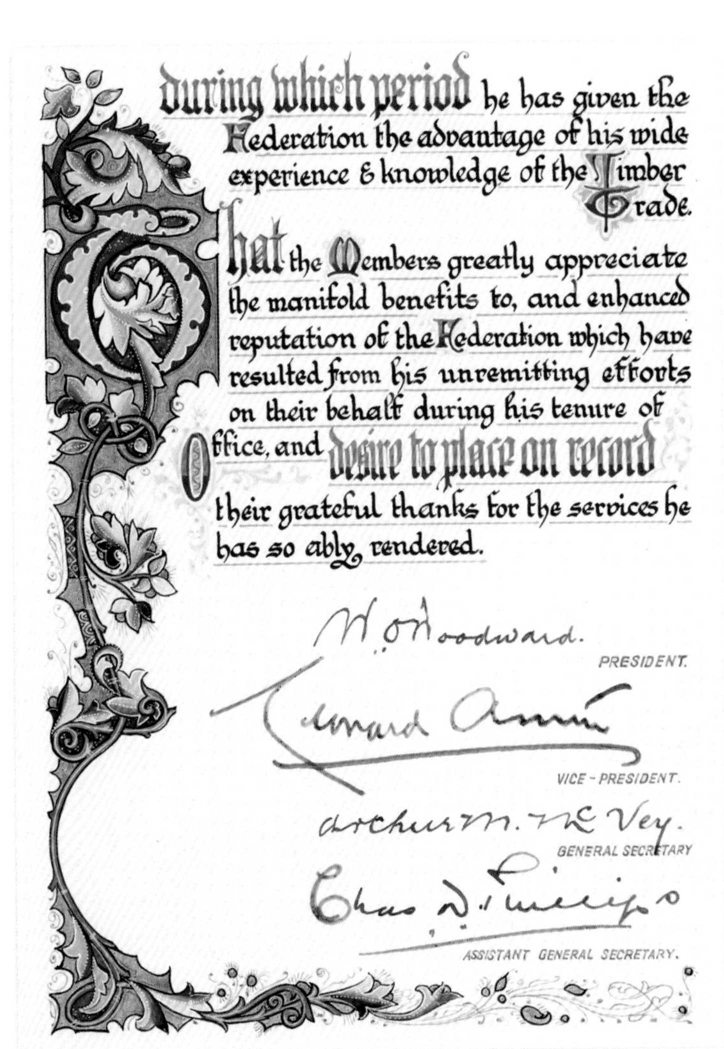

during which period he has given the Federation the advantage of his wide experience & knowledge of the Timber Trade.

That the Members greatly appreciate the manifold benefits to, and enhanced reputation of the Federation which have resulted from his unremitting efforts on their behalf during his tenure of Office, and desire to place on record their grateful thanks for the services he has so ably rendered.

W. Woodward.
PRESIDENT.

VICE-PRESIDENT.

Archer M. McVey.
GENERAL SECRETARY

Chas. D. Phillips
ASSISTANT GENERAL SECRETARY.

Pages 4 and 5 of the address to
Major Archibald Isidore Harris given in 1939.

University of Leeds professor
Professor Norman Mederson Comber DSc, ARCS, FRIC

In 1953 Professor Noman Mederson Comber was thanked on his retirement for his twenty-one years of service from 1932–53 as President of the Leeds University Union Agricultural Society.

He had other roles within the university, including twenty-five years on the Senate, Dean of the Faculty of Technology and Chairman of the Board of the Faculties of Science and Technology. He had academic involvement outside the university, including President of the Agricultural Section of the British Association, and was the author of *An Introduction to the Scientific Study of the Soil*, published in 1927.

Within this simple address are twenty-one typed pages of the names and addresses of staff and current and previous students, followed by their signatures. Clearly, this was a man much loved by his students, friends and colleagues. Sadly, Professor Comber died within three months of his retirement as Professor of Agricultural Chemistry and Head of the Department of Agriculture. He left a widow and two children.

Comber was brought up in Brighton and studied chemistry at the Royal College of Science in London. His first job was with the East Anglican Institute of Agriculture in Chelmsford, which got him interested in soil science. He joined the University of Leeds staff in 1913, becoming the Chair of Agricultural Chemistry in 1924. He was very active in many roles within the university and outside it, including helping to establish the Yorkshire Federation of Young Farmers' Clubs. He was also President of the Yorkshire Association of Baptist Churches.

The address to Professor Norman Mederson Comber, DSc, ARCS, FRIC given in 1953.

Leeds University Union Agricultural Society

to

Professor N. M. Comber

President of the Society

1932 ~ 1953

Club president
Sir John D. Laurie, TD, JP

Colonel and Alderman Sir John D. Laurie, TD, JP, was President of the City Livery Club from 1937–8. He was also a liveryman, Past Prime Warden of the Worshipful Company of Saddlers and Liveryman and Past Master of the Worshipful Company of Woolmen.

Sir John D. Laurie.

Sir John's neat illuminated address was presented to him on the termination of his office as President of the City Livery Club, together with a Past President's badge. The presentation was made by Sidney J. Fox as the first duty of the newly elected President. However, Sir John had to return the illuminated address for it to be subsequently incorporated into a bound volume of *The Liveryman*, the club's magazine.

The bound book includes five editions of the magazine from October 1937–8, the year book and the list of club members. The October 1938 edition includes both a photograph of the illumination and a write-up of the presentational speeches.

Sir John was a stockbroker, being the Senior Partner in Laurie, Millbank & Co. of Birchin Lane, London. He was alderman for the Ward of Cornhill from 1931, after the death of Sir William Waterlow, Bt. In 1935 he was Senior Sheriff of the City of London and Lord Mayor of London in 1941. His grandfather had been a sheriff in 1849, and his great uncle had been a sheriff in 1823 and Lord Mayor in 1832. Sir John was knighted in 1936.

Colonel and Alderman
Sir John D. Laurie,
T.D., J.P.
Liveryman of the Worshipful Companies of
Saddlers Past Prime Warden.
and
Woolmen Past Master.

The Members of the City Livery Club, desire to express to you on the termination of your year of Office as President their cordial appreciation of the services you have rendered during the past twelve months.

Your great interest, earnestness, sincerity, and the manner in which you have presided over the deliberations of the Council with distinction have added dignity and prestige to the Club and enhanced its reputation.

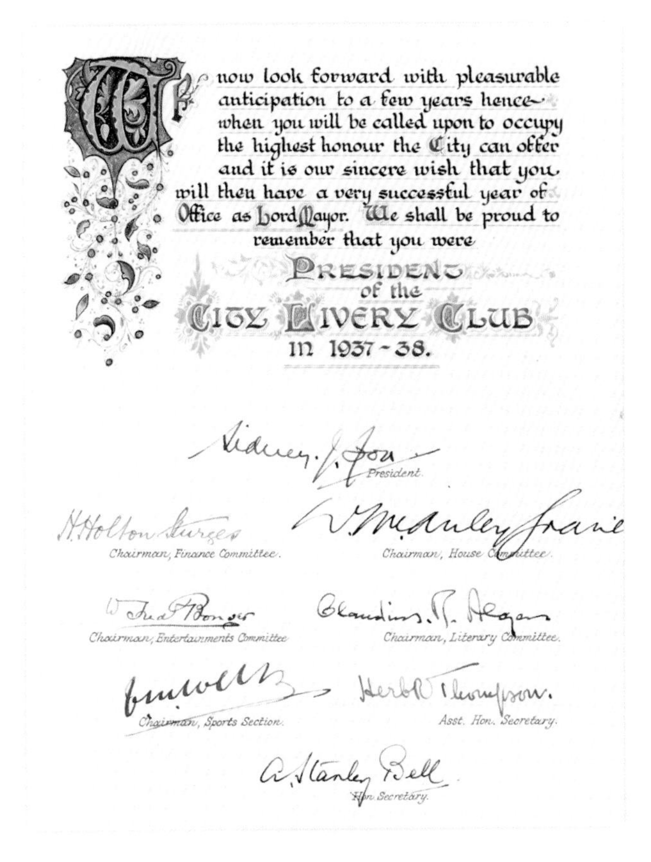

We now look forward with pleasurable anticipation to a few years hence when you will be called upon to occupy the highest honour the City can offer and it is our sincere wish that you will then have a very successful year of Office as Lord Mayor. We shall be proud to remember that you were
President of the City Livery Club in 1937-38.

Sidney J. Fox, President.
Chairman, Finance Committee.
Chairman, House Committee.
Chairman, Entertainments Committee.
Chairman, Literary Committee.
Chairman, Sports Section.
Herbert Thompson, Asst. Hon. Secretary.
A. Stanley Bell, Hon. Secretary.

The address to Sir John D. Laurie given in 1938.

Sir John had fought in the Boer War, commanding a battalion of the West Kents, and he was mentioned in dispatches in the First World War while fighting in France and Belgium.

Sir John was a resident of Sevenoaks and was widely involved in local affairs. For twenty-one years he was a member of the Sevenoaks Urban District Council and the chairman three times. His many other roles included President of Sevenoaks and District Football League and President of Sevenoaks Football Club.

Patternmaker
William Mosses

The United Pattern Makers Association of Manchester awarded William Mosses with a colourful, professional illuminated address with fine gold highlighting and design in 1912 for his twenty-eight years of service as General Secretary.

Mosses was actually General Secretary of the United Pattern Makers Association until 1917, so it is not clear why he was given an award in 1912. Perhaps it was because the association moved its headquarters to London in that year.

Mosses was also active in the Trades Union Congress (TUC) movement. He was a member of the Parliamentary Committee twice and one of the TUC representatives at the American Federation of Labour (the American equivalent of the TUC) in 1905.

He was also the first General Secretary of the Federation of Engineering and Shipbuilding Trades from 1890.

A patternmaker makes patterns on materials. It is a skilled job, based in different industries such as clothing or metalwork. A designer outlines a pattern and the patternmaker converts the design into an object, which could be made of wood, metal, cloth or other material depending on the product. Sometimes patterns are created by making cuts into the material so that the pattern is incised. The patternmaker needs to be highly skilled in materials, design and engineering.
In Mosses' time these skills would have been learned through an apprenticeship.

Page 1 of the address to William Mosses given in 1912, illuminated by Kelsall, 11 Cloisters Street, Bolton.

United Pattern Makers' Association

To

Mr. Wm. Mosses

Manchester, July 12th. 1912.

Dear Sir & Brother,

The Officers and Members of the above Association are desirous of recording in some permanent manner their sincere appreciation of the very able services you have rendered as General Secretary during the past twenty-eight years.

The untiring energy and zeal with which you have carried out the work - your strength of character and sterling integrity in thought and action, have, without doubt, been largely instrumental in raising the Society from a position of comparative obscurity, to one of great influence in the engineering world.

DEATH

A death in America
Eugene Van Rensselaer Thayer Jr

This illuminated address shows that illuminated presentations are not unique to the UK. The small illumination comprises of six pages of fine calligraphy embellished with neat and tasteful illuminated letters. It was produced by B.C. Kassell Co., Chicago, Illinois.

This illuminated presentation is a rare example of a sad occasion as, normally, illuminated addresses celebrate a happy event. The booklet was presented to Thayer Jr's family following his death in 1937, in recognition of his service as a director of the Terminal National Bank of Chicago. The other eleven directors of the bank are all named.

Thayer Jr was born in 1881 in Boston, Massachusetts, the son of Eugene and Susan. He married twice. His first marriage was to Gladys Baldwin Brooks in 1903, but they divorced in 1923. His second marriage was to Mary Elizabeth Harding.

Thayer Jr went to Harvard in 1904 and by 1912 had become President of the Merchants National Bank of Boston. He then became President of the Chase National Bank in New York and a director of numerous other companies, including Coca-Cola.

His ancestry appears to derive from Nathaniel Thayer who was born in Thornbury, Gloucestershire, England in 1639 and died in Braintree, Massachusetts.

The Thayer family is well represented in American history, including: Colonel Sylvanus Thayer, who established the curriculum for West Point Military Academy, is known as the Father of the Military Academy and has a monument on the campus; a number of

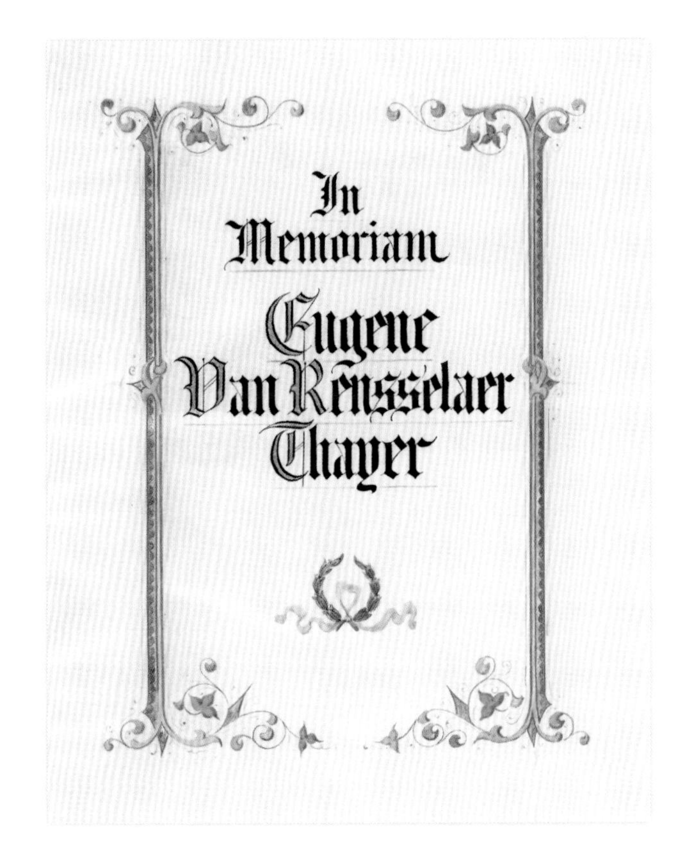

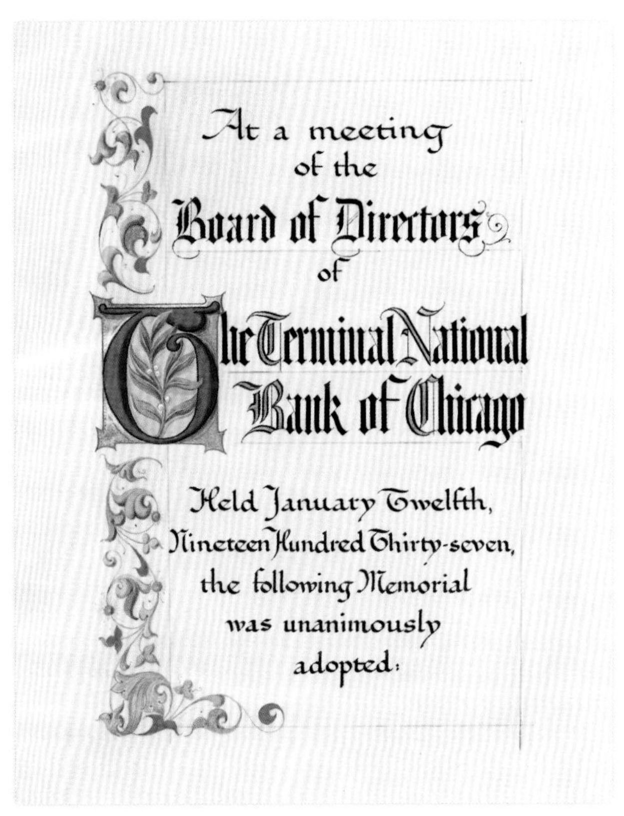

Pages 1 and 2 of the address in respect of Eugene Van Rensselaer Thayer Jr given in 1937, illuminated by B.C. Kassell Co., Chicago.

members of the House of Representatives; William Wallace Thayer, a Governor of Oregon; Samuel R. Thayer, US Ambassador to the Netherlands; Edwin Pope Thayer, member as the Senate; and John Borland Thayer and his son, Jack who were passengers on the *Titanic*.

hereas, In His
Infinite wisdom,
God has removed
from his family,
his friends and associates,

Eugene Van Rensselaer Thayer

And Whereas, he was a
distinguished and val-
ued former member of the
Board of Directors of this
Bank, esteemed and beloved
by his fellow directors as a
man of character and integ-
rity. In the days of stress,
because of his broad and

mature experience, his high ideals and kindly personality, he contributed immeasurably to the stabilization of our Bank, and

Whereas, in his passing, our Bank has lost a wise and sincere counsellor, his family a devoted father and husband, and the country a patriotic and philanthropic citizen; *Now, Therefore, Be it*

Resolved, that we hereby profess admiration and affection for him and his sterling qualities of mind and character, as well as our deep and abiding sense of loss in his passing, ∗∗∗

And be it further

Resolved, That this Resolution be spread at large upon the Minute Book of the Bank, and an engrossed copy delivered to his family, with sincerest expressions of sympathy and condolence.

President

Pages 3, 4 and 5 of the address in respect of Eugene Van Rensselaer Thayer Jr given in 1937.

ESTATE OWNERS

Explorer
Henry M. Stanley

Henry M. Stanley is famous for his attributed quote 'Dr Livingstone, I presume?' Many readers may also know him as a journalist. Therefore, it may be surprising to find him included in an illuminated address list, with an address linked to his visit to the Haddo Estate, the home of Lord and Lady Aberdeen.

This large illuminated picture is more a curio than a beautiful work of art. It appears to have been presented by the tenants of the Haddo Estate, although the date is not given. Unfortunately, the ink signatures have faded over the course of time.

The picture celebrates, in elaborate language, Stanley's visit and honours his 'heroic labours in the field of African Exploration' and 'heroic career'.

Stanley was born in Wales to unmarried parents in 1841. In his early life he was known as John Rowlands and he lived with his grandfather until his death, then with other relatives and then in the poor workhouse in St Asaph, Denbighshire. When he was eighteen he went to the United States, arriving in New Orleans where he found a local trader, Henry H. Stanley, willing to employ him. They got on well and the trader became a father figure, to the point at which John Rowlands changed his name to Henry Morton Stanley. He was a soldier in the Civil War, firstly for the Confederates and later, briefly, for the Union before becoming a sailor in the Union Navy. On board, he took the role of messenger which subsequently led to his interest in being a journalist.

His journalism involved acting as a correspondent at the Indian Peace Commission, and this led to him working exclusively for the *New York Herald*. He became the *Herald*'s overseas correspondent and was sent in

The address to
Henry M. Stanley.

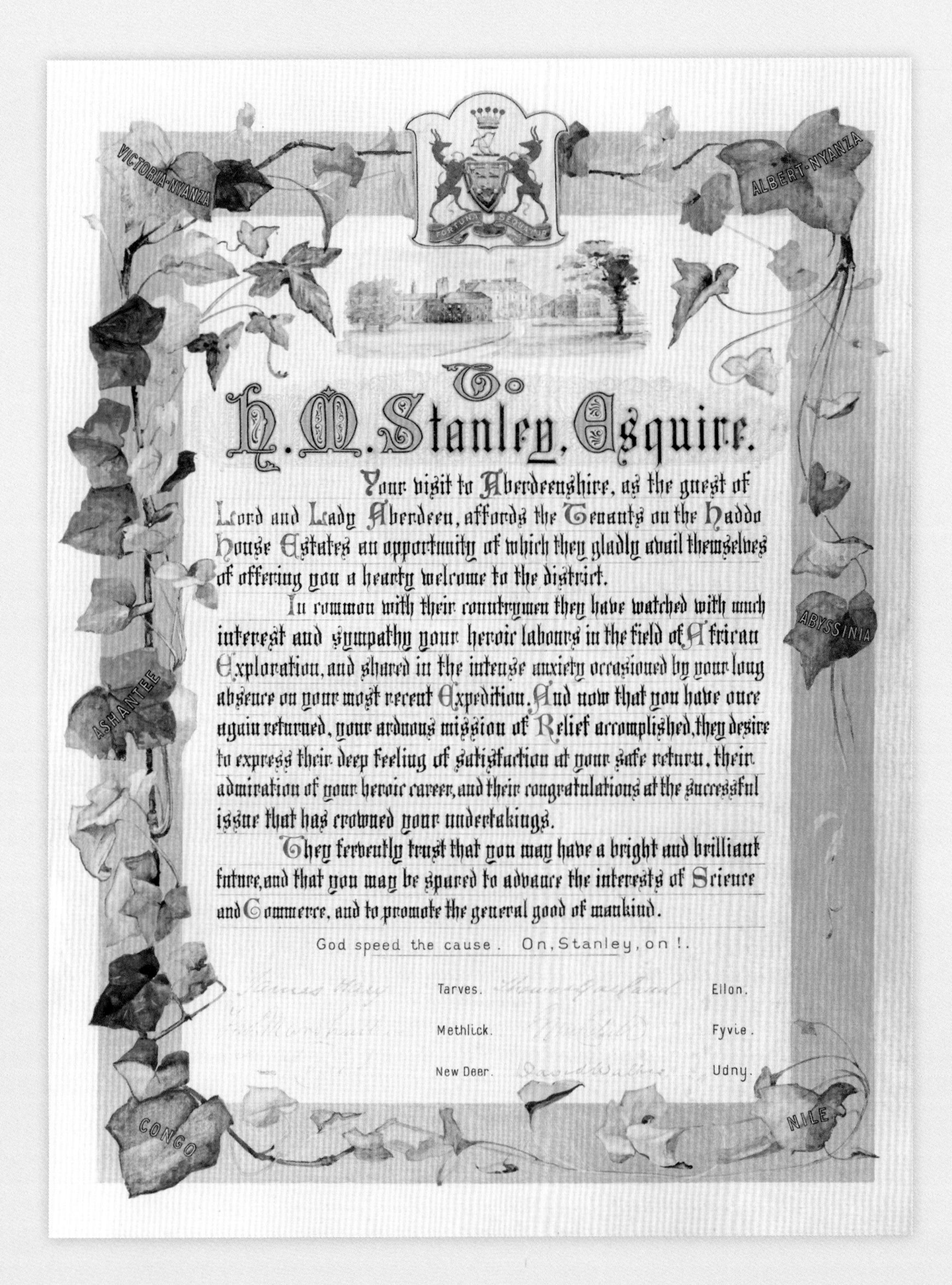

To

H. M. Stanley, Esquire.

Your visit to Aberdeenshire, as the guest of Lord and Lady Aberdeen, affords the Tenants on the Haddo House Estates an opportunity of which they gladly avail themselves of offering you a hearty welcome to the district.

In common with their countrymen they have watched with much interest and sympathy your heroic labours in the field of African Exploration, and shared in the intense anxiety occasioned by your long absence on your most recent Expedition. And now that you have once again returned, your arduous mission of Relief accomplished, they desire to express their deep feeling of satisfaction at your safe return, their admiration of your heroic career, and their congratulations at the successful issue that has crowned your undertakings.

They fervently trust that you may have a bright and brilliant future, and that you may be spared to advance the interests of Science and Commerce, and to promote the general good of mankind.

God speed the cause. On, Stanley, on !.

Tarves. Ellon.

Methlick. Fyvie.

New Deer. Udny.

1869 to find Dr David Livingstone. He travelled to Zanzibar in 1871 to collect provisions for his exploration. He found Dr Livingstone in late 1871 near Lake Tanganyika. The greeting 'Dr Livingstone, I presume?' is not corroborated by reports, and is likely to have been created editorially later for publication in the *New York Herald*.

David Livingstone was born in 1813 in Scotland and is famous for having been a doctor, missionary and explorer. His exploits were popular with the public. He was keen to find the source of the Nile, as he thought it would give him valuable influence in his missionary work. While in Africa he lost contact with the outside world for six years, until found by Stanley. He died in Africa.

Lord Aberdeen, referred to in the address, is likely to have been John Campbell Hamilton-Gordon, 1st Marquess of Aberdeen and Temair, and the 7th Earl of Aberdeen. He was a politician, Lord Lieutenant of Ireland and Governor General of Canada. His father had been the 5th Earl, who died in 1864, and his older brother had been the 6th Earl until his death in 1870. Lady Aberdeen was Ishbel Maria Marjoribanks, daughter to Sir Dudley Marjoribanks, the 1st Baron Tweedmouth.

The 4th Earl, who also had lived on the Haddo Estate, was the British Prime Minister from 1852–5. The Haddo Estate is now owned by the National Trust for Scotland.

A well-connected family
The Hon. Charles Forbes-Trefusis

Here there are two illuminated scrolls for The Hon. Charles Forbes-Trefusis.

The first illuminated scroll was given to The Hon. Charles Forbes-Trefusis of Pitsligo, Fettercairn and Invermay, in Scotland by the tenants, feuars and other residents of New Pitsligo in 1884 on attaining his majority. Feuars is a Scottish word for people who use land in return for a fee or service, with a similar usage as feudal.

The Hon. Charles John Robert Hepburn-Stuart-Forbes-Trefusis was the son of the 20th Baron Clinton and succeeded to the title in 1904. He had many roles, including Keeper of the Privy Seal of the Duchy of Cornwall, Lord Warden of the Stannaries, Joint Parliamentary Secretary to the Board of Agriculture and Fisheries, Chairman of the Forestry Commission and a director of Southern Railways.

Forbes-Trefusis's mother was Harriet Forbes, daughter of Sir John Stuart Hepburn Forbes, 8th Baronet of Monymusk, Fettercairn and Pitsligo. His maternal and paternal grandmothers were related, being sisters Elizabeth and Harriett Kerr.

Forbes-Trefusis was married to Lady Jane McDonnell, daughter and one of the ten children of Mark McDonnell, the 5th Earl of Antrim. Mark McDowell was the son of Lord Mark Kerr, a descendant of the Marquess of Lothian and Charlotte McDonnell, the Countess of Antrim.

The second illuminated scroll was given to Forbes-Trefusis in 1885 in gratitude for standing in the General Election on behalf of the Unionists of Kincardineshire.

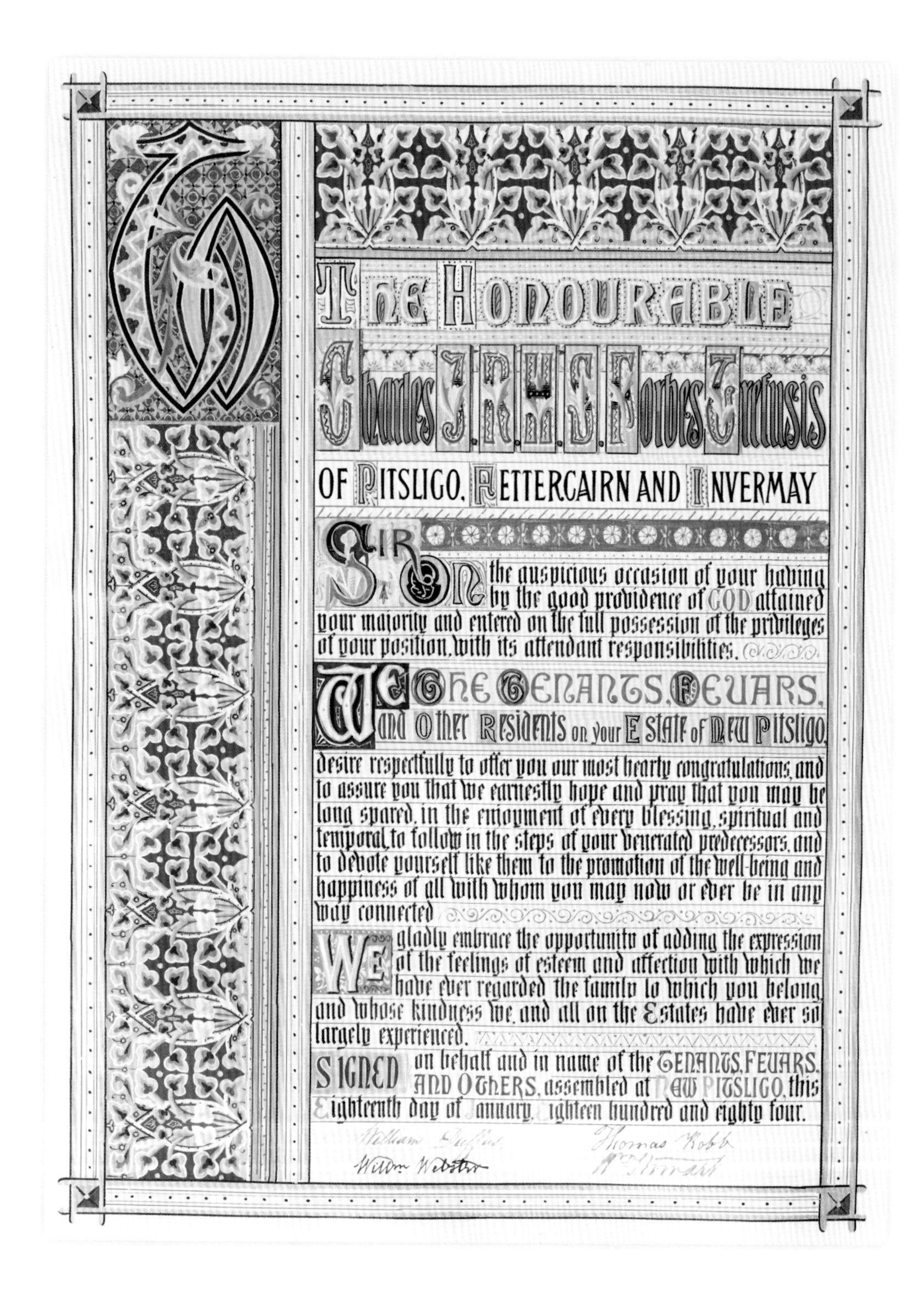

To

The Honourable
Charles J. R. H. S. Forbes Trefusis
of Pitsligo, Fettercairn and Invermay

Sir,

On the auspicious occasion of your having by the good providence of GOD attained your majority and entered on the full possession of the privileges of your position, with its attendant responsibilities,

We the Tenants, Feuars, and other Residents on your Estate of New Pitsligo, desire respectfully to offer you our most hearty congratulations, and to assure you that we earnestly hope and pray that you may be long spared, in the enjoyment of every blessing, spiritual and temporal, to follow in the steps of your venerated predecessors, and to devote yourself like them to the promotion of the well-being and happiness of all with whom you may now or ever be in any way connected.

We gladly embrace the opportunity of adding the expression of the feelings of esteem and affection with which we have ever regarded the family to which you belong, and whose kindness we, and all on the Estates have ever so largely experienced.

Signed on behalf and in name of the Tenants, Feuars, and Others, assembled at New Pitsligo, this Eighteenth day of January, Eighteen hundred and eighty four.

Thomas Robb

He inherited the 55,000 acres of the Rolle estates in Devon, in 1907, including Stevenstone House in Great Torrington, the grand family home of the Rolle family. Forbes-Trefusis inherited the estates form his uncle Mark Rolle, who had inherited the estates from his uncle and aunt, John Rolle, 1st Baron Rolle and his wife Louisa who had been Louisa Trefusis before marriage, daughter of an earlier Baron Clinton. Forbes-Trefusis sold Stevenstone in 1912 to Captain John Oliver Clemson and his wife Mary. The captain died at Gallipoli in 1915 and Mary remarried.

Stevenstone was auctioned twice, in 1930 and 1931, and the estate was sold in pieces and gradually demolished. Stevenstone's library still stands and can be rented for holidays from the Landmark Trust.

The Hon. Charles Forbes-Trefusis, 21st Baron Clinton, had two daughters. One, the Hon. Fenella Hepburn Stuart Forbes-Trefusis married the Hon. John Herbert Bowes-Lyon, the son of the 14th Earl of Strathmore and Kinghorne and brother to Elizabeth Bowes-Lyon, who became Queen Elizabeth, mother to Queen Elizabeth II.

Stevenstone House.

The address to the Hon. Charles Forbes-Trefusis given in 1884.

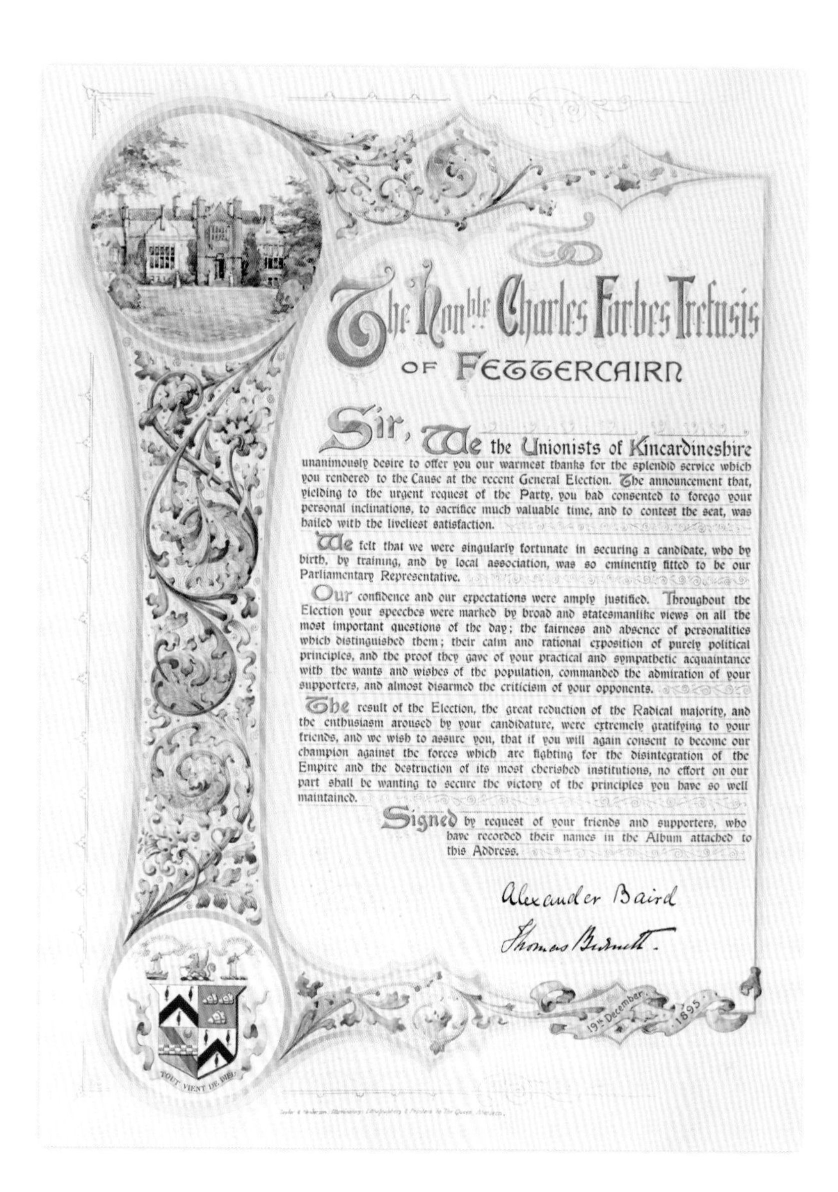

The Hon^ble Charles Forbes-Trefusis
of Fettercairn

Sir, We the Unionists of Kincardineshire unanimously desire to offer you our warmest thanks for the splendid service which you rendered to the Cause at the recent General Election. The announcement that, yielding to the urgent request of the Party, you had consented to forego your personal inclinations, to sacrifice much valuable time, and to contest the seat, was hailed with the liveliest satisfaction.

We felt that we were singularly fortunate in securing a candidate, who by birth, by training, and by local association, was so eminently fitted to be our Parliamentary Representative.

Our confidence and our expectations were amply justified. Throughout the Election your speeches were marked by broad and statesmanlike views on all the most important questions of the day; the fairness and absence of personalities which distinguished them; their calm and rational exposition of purely political principles, and the proof they gave of your practical and sympathetic acquaintance with the wants and wishes of the population, commanded the admiration of your supporters, and almost disarmed the criticism of your opponents.

The result of the Election, the great reduction of the Radical majority, and the enthusiasm aroused by your candidature, were extremely gratifying to your friends, and we wish to assure you, that if you will again consent to become our champion against the forces which are fighting for the disintegration of the Empire and the destruction of its most cherished institutions, no effort on our part shall be wanting to secure the victory of the principles you have so well maintained.

Signed by request of your friends and supporters, who have recorded their names in the Album attached to this Address.

Alexander Baird

Thomas Burnett.

19th December 1895

The aaddress to the Hon. Charles Forbes-Trefusis given in 1885, illuminated by Taylor & Henderson, Aberdeen.

If you are a folk dance enthusiast you may recognise the name Trefusis. There is a Trefusis Hall within Cecil Sharp House in London named after Lady Mary Hepburn Stuart Forbes-Trefusis (sister-in-law to Forbes-Trefusis). Cecil Sharp House is the home of the English Folk Dance Society and Lady Mary was their President from 1913 until her death in 1927.

Brewer
Robert Blezard

Robert Blezard lived at Pool Park in Ruthin, Denbighshire, North Wales. His son George celebrated his twenty-first birthday in 1876 and the residents of Ruthin took the opportunity to congratulate Blezard for his son attaining the age of majority with the presentation of a single page, rather formal address with gold embellishing. They did so because the Blezard family provided employment and support for the community.

The cover of the illuminated folder.

Pool Park is on the site of one of the deer parks of Ruthin Castle. The estate was in the ownership of the Salesbury family until it passed by marriage to the Bagot family in 1670. The story goes that Sir Walter Bagot's spaniel strayed on to Jane Salesbury's land and he instantly fell in love with Jane, who was a wealthy heiress. Their marriage took place in secret and Jane's cousin William spent the rest of his life contesting Jane's inheritance, without success.

The estate remained in the Bagot family and the house was rebuilt in 1826. Later in the nineteenth century the estate was let out. George Richards Elkington, who pioneered electroplating, was a tenant, and died there in 1865. Later Blezard, a brewer, took the tenancy. Robert and George both bred a herd of shorthorn cows on the estate. George died there in 1907.

In 1928 Pool Park was lost to the Bagot family on a bet at the races and the estate was put on the market. The parkland was sold to a timber merchant and some of the tenant farmers bought their farms.

To Robert Blezard Esq,
Pool Park, Ruthin.

Dear Sir,

There is a general feeling among the inhabitants of Ruthin that they cannot permit the majority of your only Son Mr George Blezard, to take place without offering you their sincere congratulations on this auspicious event, and wishing you and your son the enjoyment during many future years of health and happiness.

During your residence at Pool Park you have earned the esteem and respect of all classes of Society. Your kindness of heart and liberality are well known and highly appreciated Seldom if ever has an application been made to you in vain to render succour to those who need it or to assist in promoting a worthy cause.

We have every reason to anticipate that your Son will follow the example of his Father and be equally esteemed and beloved with yourself We sincerely trust that he may be spared by Providence to live a useful and honorable life.

We remain, Dear Sir,
Faithfully Yours,

Signed on behalf of the Inhabitants of Ruthin by

R. [illegible] Ellis, Chairman of Committee.
[illegible] Secretary.

Ruthin Feby 23rd 1876.

[illegible] GREEN, RUTHIN

The house was leased to Sir Ernest Tate, 3rd Baronet, as a retreat. Sir Ernest Tate was the grandson of Sir Henry Tate, 1st Baronet, of Tate & Lyle, the sugar manufacturer. Sir Henry Tate had created a sugar refining business in Liverpool in 1859, and it expanded into East London, based at Silvertown, in 1878. On his death in 1899 he donated his collection of paintings to the nation, now held in the Tate Gallery.

In 1934 Pool Park was converted to a convalescent home. The grounds were used as a prisoner of war camp during the Second World War. After the war the house became a mental hospital until 1989. It was sold in 1992 and has remained empty ever since.

The address to Robert Blezard given in 1876, illuminated by W. Green, Ruthin.

An inheritance
William Egerton Garnett-Botfield

William Egerton Garnett-Botfield was given a large, impressive folder housing an illuminated address by the tenants of his father's estate, Decker Hall, Shifnal in Shropshire on the occasion of his marriage.

The illuminated address is undated and his wife is not named, but we know from other sources that he married Elizabeth Clulow Howard-McLean of Aston Hall in 1881.

Garnett-Botfield was the eldest son and one of six children born in 1849 to the Rev. William Bishton Garnett-Botfield and his wife Sarah Dutton. He was born in Findon, Sussex. His father inherited an estate and fortune in 1863, and took the name Botfield by Royal Licence.

Garnett-Botfield had three children. He was a magistrate, councillor, alderman and mayor, and gave much support to local schools. He died at The Hut, Bishop's Castle in Shropshire in 1906.

Cover of the illuminated address.

Page 1 of the address to William Egerton Garnett-Botfield, most likely given in 1911, illuminated by Adnitt & Naunton, Salop.

TO
WILLIAM EGERTON
GARNETT BOTFIELD
ESQUIRE
ADNITT & NAUNTON, ILLUMINATORS, SALOP.

Dear Sir,

We the undersigned Tenants on your Father's Estate desirous of testifying our interest in your welfare and happiness take this earliest opportunity of offering you our most sincere congratulations on the joyous occasion of your marriage with the Lady in whom your choice has commended to our regard and esteem. So important an event we need hardly say have been looked forward to by us with the greatest interest and which we trust will be as productive of

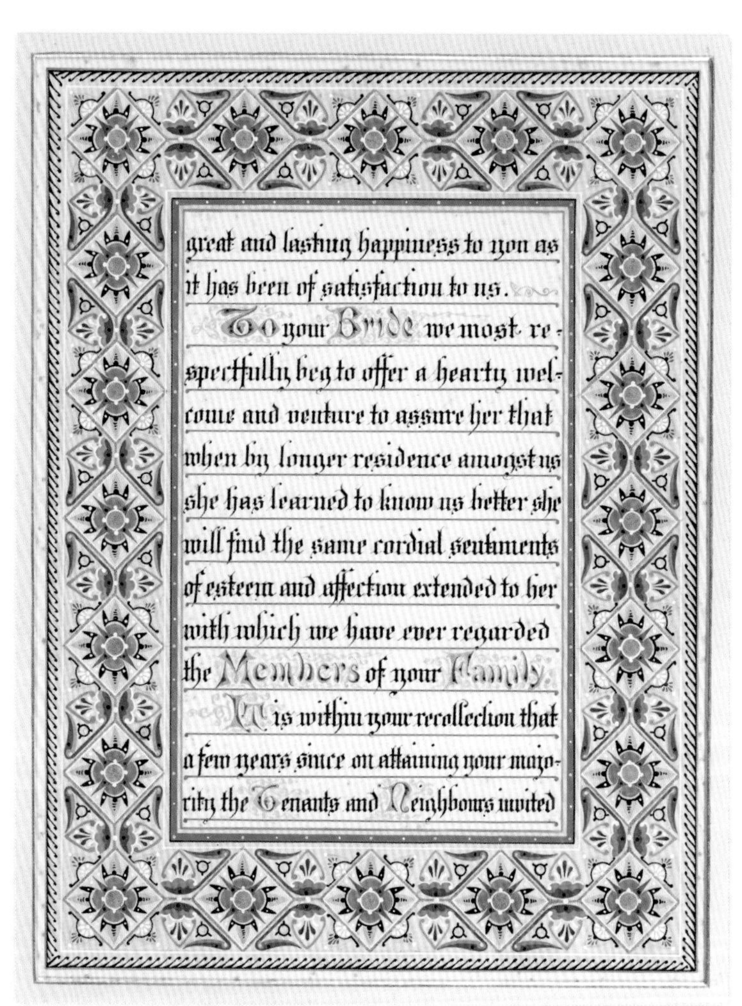

great and lasting happiness to you as it has been of satisfaction to us.

To your Bride we most respectfully beg to offer a hearty welcome and venture to assure her that when by longer residence amongst us she has learned to know us better she will find the same cordial sentiments of esteem and affection extended to her with which we have ever regarded the Members of your Family.

It is within your recollection that a few years since on attaining your majority the Tenants and Neighbours invited

Pages 2 and 3 of the address to William Egerton Garnett-Botfield, most likely given in 1911.

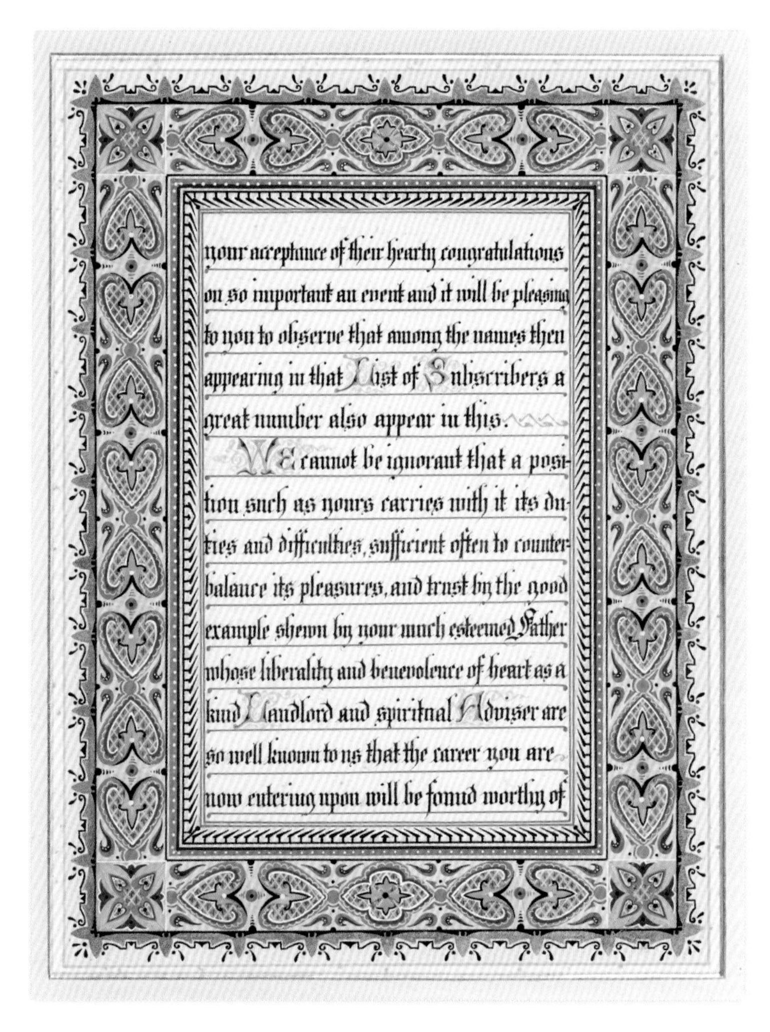

your acceptance of their hearty congratulations
on so important an event and it will be pleasing
to you to observe that among the names then
appearing in that List of Subscribers a
great number also appear in this.
WE cannot be ignorant that a posi-
tion such as yours carries with it its du-
ties and difficulties, sufficient often to counter-
balance its pleasures, and trust by the good
example shewn by your much esteemed Father
whose liberality and benevolence of heart as a
kind Landlord and spiritual Adviser are
so well known to us that the career you are
now entering upon will be found worthy of

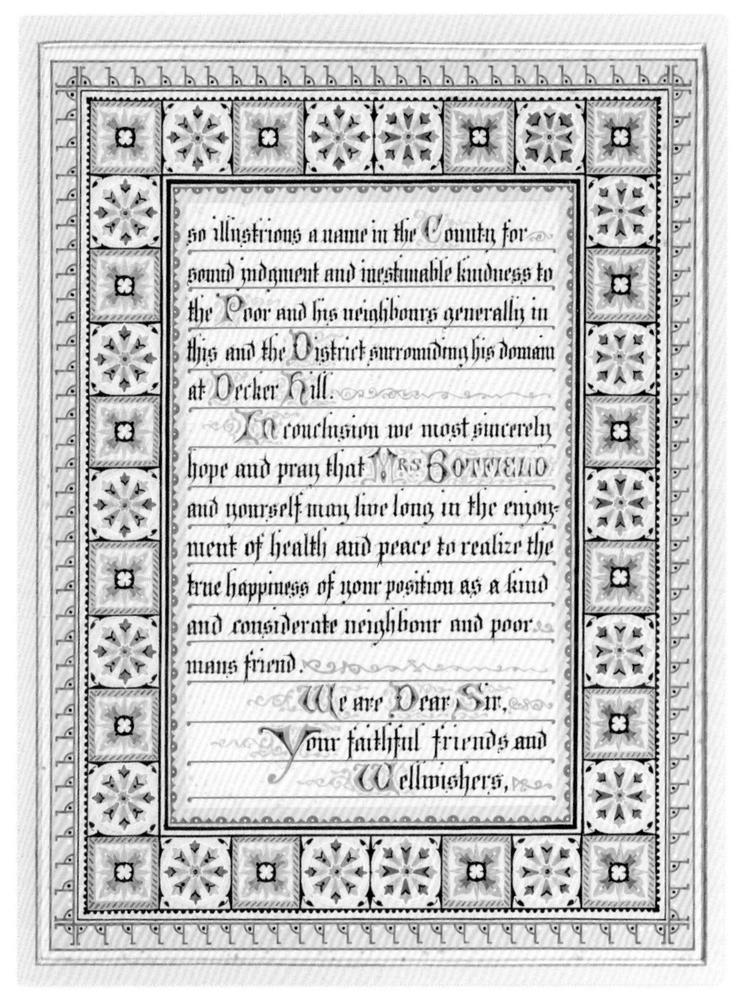

so illustrious a name in the County for
sound judgment and inestimable kindness to
the Poor and his neighbours generally in
this and the District surrounding his domain
at Decker Hill.
In conclusion we most sincerely
hope and pray that Mrs Botfield
and yourself may live long in the enjoy-
ment of health and peace to realize the
true happiness of your position as a kind
and considerate neighbour and poor
mans friend.
We are Dear Sir,
Your faithful friends and
Wellwishers,

Pages 4 and 5 of the address to William Egerton Garnett-Botfield, most likely given in 1911.

MARRIAGE

Marriage in Daventry
Mr and Mrs Herbert Mountain

It is a unique gift to give an original illuminated presentation. The members of the Christian Endeavour Society in Daventry presented both a tea service and a small, humble booklet housing the illuminated address when Herbert Mountain married Miss Simpson to become Mr and Mrs Mountain in June 1912. It is pleasing to see ordinary, as well as titled, people receiving an illuminated address.

This is a short and simple but very effective modern-looking design in the Art Nouveau style, which had developed in the late 1800s, taking its design from the natural shape of flowers and plants and using whiplash lines. These are evident in the colourful surrounds to the text.

I had wondered whether Herbert's parents had been influenced by the early nineteenth-century polar expeditions in naming their son, as the Herbert Mountains are a mountain range in Antarctica, but this was not the case. The Herbert Mountains were named in 1957 after being identified by an expedition led by Sir Edwin Herbert.

The address to Mr and Mrs Herbert Mountain given in 1912.

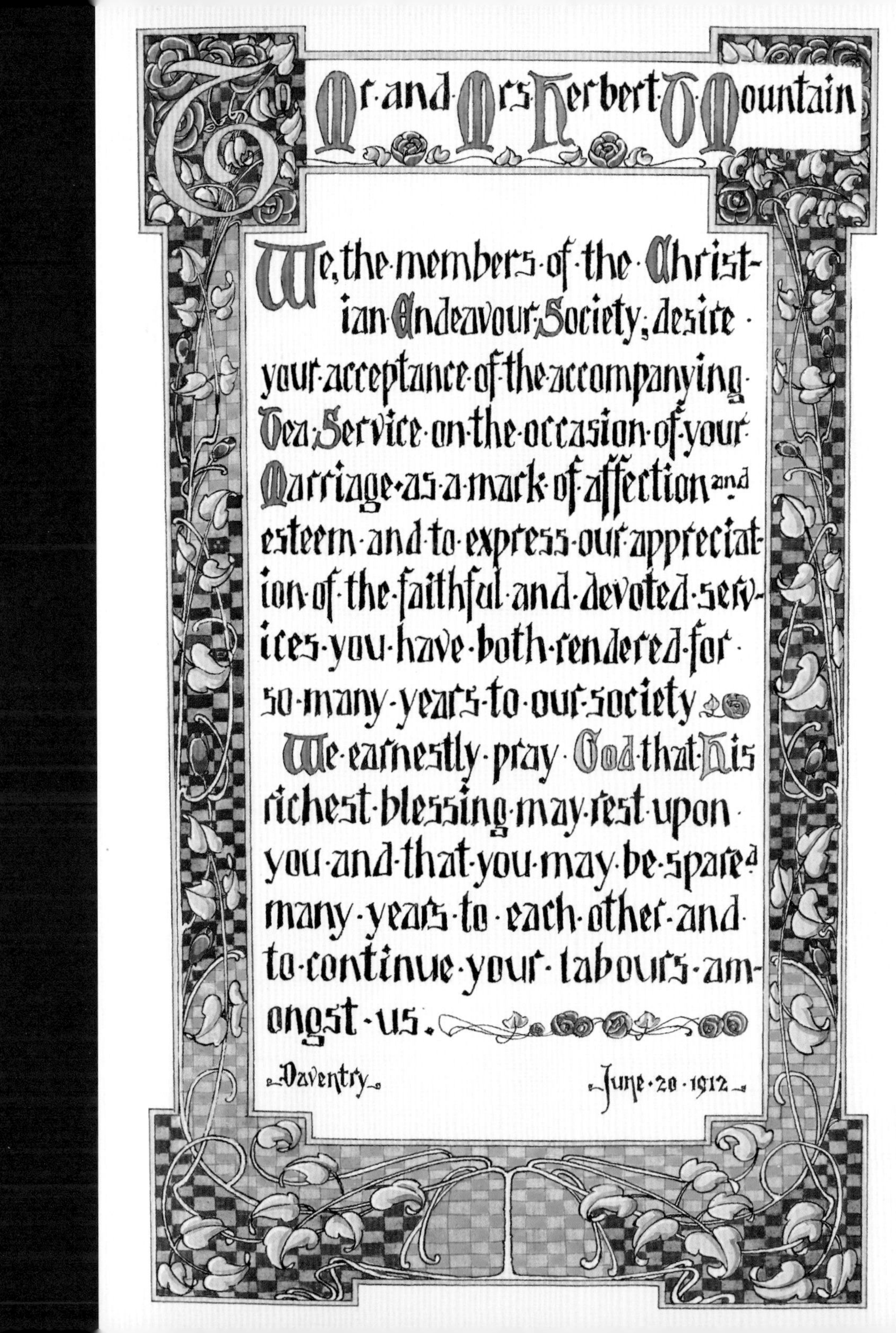

To Mr and Mrs Herbert T Mountain

We, the members of the Christian Endeavour Society, desire your acceptance of the accompanying Tea Service on the occasion of your Marriage as a mark of affection and esteem and to express our appreciation of the faithful and devoted services you have both rendered for so many years to our society.

We earnestly pray God that His richest blessing may rest upon you and that you may be spared many years to each other and to continue your labours amongst us.

Daventry

June 20 1912

Wedding
Miss Phoebe Mary Vlieland

It is sometimes difficult to remember the details of one's wedding day and, in particular, the gifts received, but some gifts are so special or unusual that they are unlikely to be forgotten.

Miss Phoebe Vlieland was given a special, beautiful gift when she married Dudley Batty in June 1912 in Exeter. The gift was a vibrant illuminated folder given by the Justices of the Peace, aldermen, councillors, governors of the Royal Albert Memorial, members of the Exeter Education Committee and other City of Exeter officials, as Phoebe's father, Charles James Vlieland, had been the Mayor of Exeter in 1911. Exeter is unusual, as it was the first English town to appoint a mayor. All the officials had contributed towards the gifts, which included a silver tray and a brooch. Two of the list of officials were Sidney Snodgrass and Thomas Tickle!

Phoebe Vlieland was from quite a comfortable family. Her father was a doctor, she had three siblings and the family was looked after by three servants.

The name Vlieland, I have assumed, derives from the place Vlieland (pronounced Vlilant), an island in the Netherlands. It is one of a string of islands between the North Sea and the mainland, due north of Amsterdam. It is a little populated island, having only one village, and consists mainly of sand dunes and is usually very windy. Phoebe's great-grandfather was Dutch.

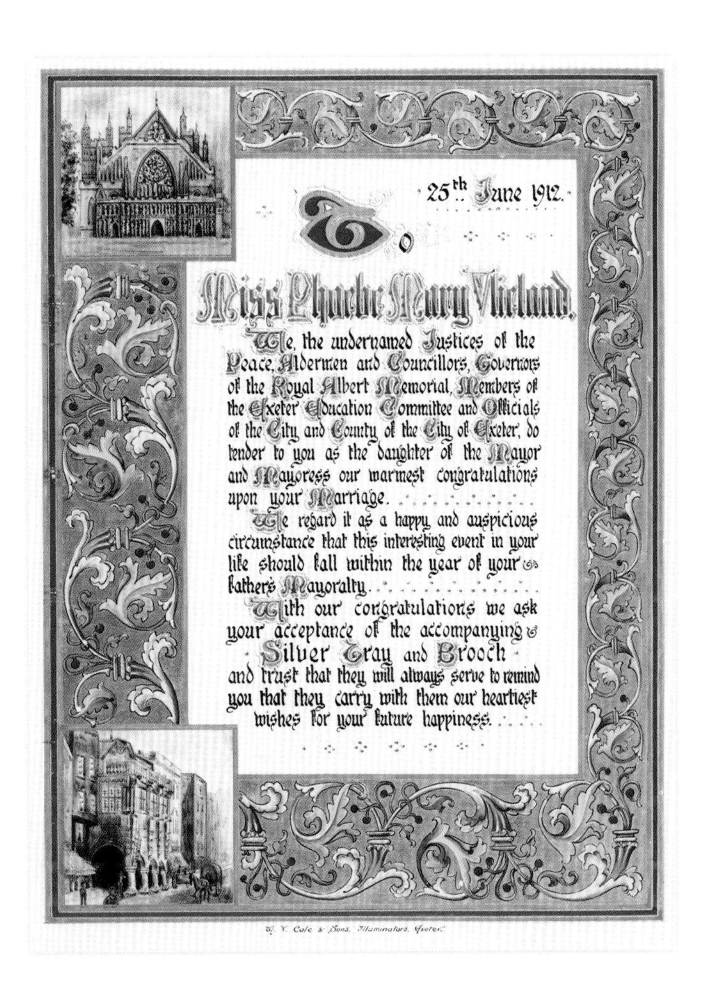

25th June 1912.

To

Miss Phoebe Mary Vlieland.

We, the undernamed Justices of the Peace, Aldermen and Councillors, Governors of the Royal Albert Memorial, Members of the Exeter Education Committee and Officials of the City and County of the City of Exeter, do tender to you as the daughter of the Mayor and Mayoress our warmest congratulations upon your Marriage.

We regard it as a happy and auspicious circumstance that this interesting event in your life should fall within the year of your father's Mayoralty.

With our congratulations we ask your acceptance of the accompanying Silver Tray and Brooch and trust that they will always serve to remind you that they carry with them our heartiest wishes for your future happiness.

The address to Phoebe Vlieland given in 1912, illuminated by W.V. Cole & Sons, Exeter.

Phoebe's husband was fifteen years her senior. He was a mechanical engineer who worked in later life for AEI (Associated Electrical Industries), an innovative scientific company. Dudley and his brother visited Australia in 1894 where he inherited his aunt's estate. It appears he was comparatively well-off. After Phoebe and Dudley's marriage in June 1912, they settled in South Kensington, where they had one child, Aubrey. Unfortunately, she lived only a few hours. Phoebe and Dudley moved to a house called Upalong in Gerrards Cross where they remained. Dudley died in 1933 at the age of sixty and Phoebe in 1980 at the age of ninety-two.

ROYALTY

Duke
The Duke of Connaught

What must it be like being one of nine children? Being part of a large family was a far more common occurrence in Victorian times than now. The Duke of Connaught was brought up in Windsor Castle, lost his father as a child and was lined up for marriage with a princess for political alliance reasons. Further, he was part of a family with siblings squabbling over their spouses' countries of origin.

HRH Prince Arthur William Patrick Albert was born at Buckingham Palace in 1850, the seventh of Queen Victoria's nine children. He was named Arthur after the Duke of Wellington. He followed a military career and served in South Africa, Canada, Egypt and India, and rose to the rank of Field Marshal. He gained his title as Duke of Connaught and Strathearn in 1874 and also became the Earl of Sussex. He was entitled to become the Duke of Saxe-Coburg and Gotha after the death of his elder brother's son, Prince Alfred of Edinburgh in 1899, but renounced the right.

The prince married Princess Louise Margaret of Prussia and they lived in Bagshot Park, in Windsor Great Park, the current home of Prince Edward, Earl of Wessex and the Countess of Wessex. They had three children. The first child, Princess Margaret, married the Crown Prince of Sweden and had five children, including Ingrid who became the Queen of Denmark and was mother to King Carl XVI Gustaf of Sweden, Queen Margrethe of Denmark and Queen Anne-Marie of Greece.

The address to the Duke of Connaught given in 1883.

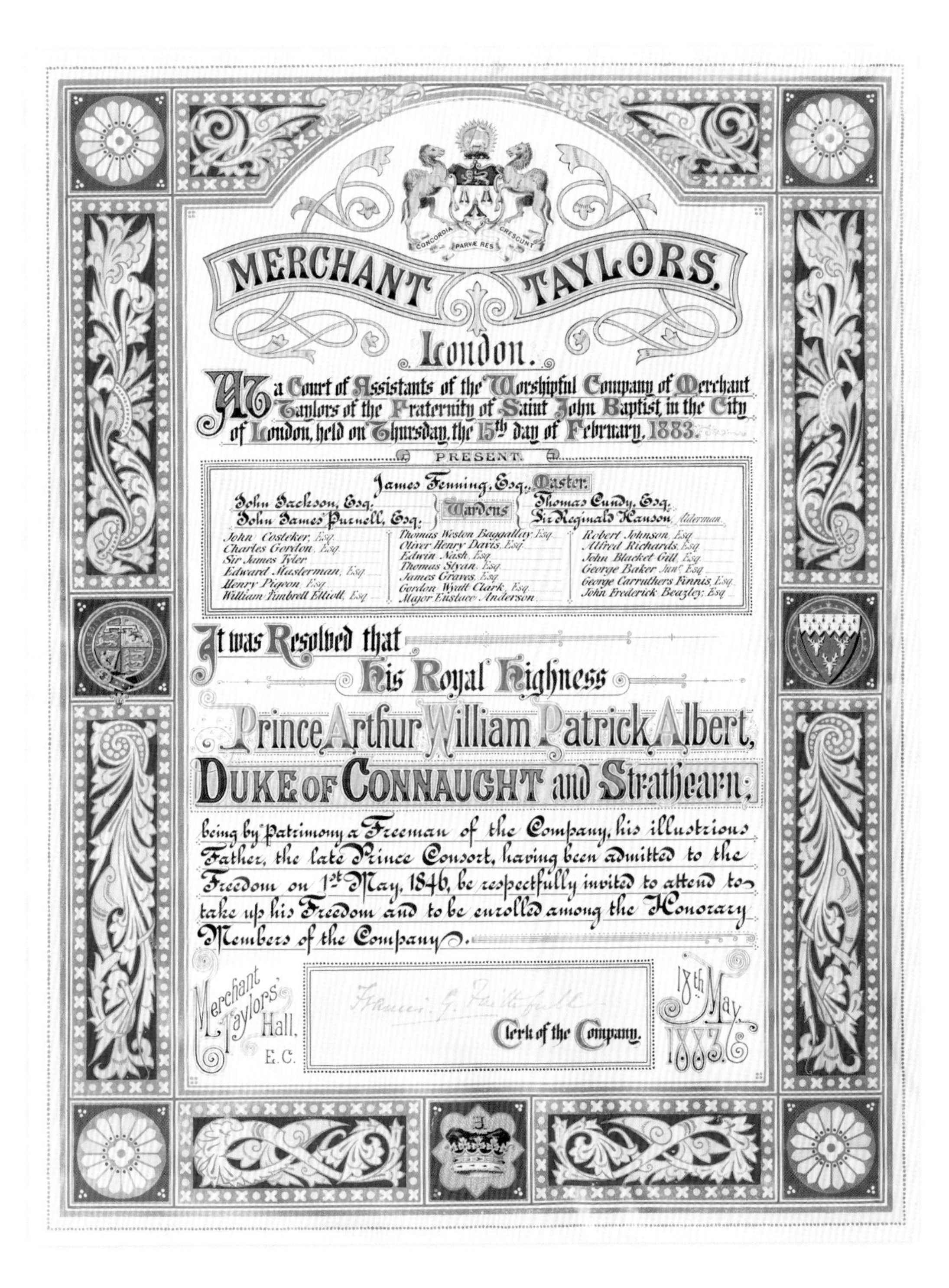

CONCORDIA PARVÆ RES CRESCUNT
MERCHANT TAYLORS.
London.
At a Court of Assistants of the Worshipful Company of Merchant Taylors of the Fraternity of Saint John Baptist, in the City of London, held on Thursday, the 15th day of February, 1883.
PRESENT.
James Fenning, Esq., Master.
John Jackson, Esq.
John James Purnell, Esq.
Wardens
Thomas Cundy, Esq.
Sir Reginald Hanson, Alderman.
John Costeker, Esq.
Charles Gordon, Esq.
Sir James Tyler
Edward Masterman, Esq.
Henry Pigeon, Esq.
William Timbrell Elliott, Esq.
Thomas Weston Baggallay, Esq.
Oliver Henry Davis, Esq.
Edwin Nash, Esq.
Thomas Styan, Esq.
James Graves, Esq.
Gordon Wyatt Clark, Esq.
Major Eustace Anderson.
Robert Johnson, Esq.
Alfred Richards, Esq.
John Blacket Gill, Esq.
George Baker Junr. Esq.
George Carruthers Finnis, Esq.
John Frederick Beazley, Esq.
It was Resolved that
His Royal Highness
Prince Arthur William Patrick Albert,
DUKE OF CONNAUGHT and Strathearn;
being by Patrimony a Freeman of the Company, his illustrious Father, the late Prince Consort, having been admitted to the Freedom on 1st May, 1846, be respectfully invited to attend to take up his Freedom and to be enrolled among the Honorary Members of the Company.
Merchant Taylors' Hall, E.C.
Clerk of the Company.
18th May 1883.

The heading of another address to the Duke of Connaught in fine illuminated lettering.

The Duke and Duchess of Connaught spent time in Canada where Prince Arthur was Governor General from 1911–16. Princess Louise died in 1917 and their daughter Princess Margaret died in 1920 whilst pregnant with her sixth child. The prince also outlived his second child, Prince Arthur, who died in 1942. The title of Duke of Connaught passed to his grandson Alastair, who died aged twenty-nine in 1943 on active service without a successor, so the title ceased.

HRH Prince Arthur William Patrick Albert Duke of Connaught and Strathearn was invited to be admitted to be enrolled as an Honorary Member of the Company of Merchant Taylors in 1883, and was given an attractive illumination to recognise this. His father, Prince Albert, had been similarly invited in 1846.

Connaught is in the west of Ireland (now renamed Connacht) and Strathearn is in Scotland.

Princess
Princess Christian of Schleswig-Holstein

The members of the royal family in Victorian and Edwardian times were probably given more illuminated presentations than anyone else. A presentation address is likely to have been given for many reasons: for a royal visit, perhaps to open a municipal building or possibly in gratitude for being a patron for a charity.

A typical, but impressive, scroll presentation was given to Princess Christian of Schleswig-Holstein in 1904 in celebration of her visit to the Royal Women's Guild of South Africa. The presentation is in private hands and I suspect that there were, and still are, too many gifts given to the royal family to be retained.

Princess Christian is liable to have gone to South Africa to visit the grave of her son, Prince Christian Victor, who had died in 1900 in the Second Boer War.

Princess Christian was born in 1846 at Buckingham Palace as HRH the Princess Helena, the fifth child of Queen Victoria and a sister to the Duke of Connaught. In 1860, when Prince Albert died, she moved with her mother and the rest of the family from Windsor Castle to Osborne House on the Isle of Wight. Helena was romantically involved with Prince Albert's librarian until he was dismissed by Queen Victoria. She welcomed and married her third cousin Prince Christian of Schleswig Holstein in 1866 at Windsor Castle, who was fifteen years her senior. As is the custom of a woman marrying a prince who has not received a peerage, she adopted her husband's Christian name as her own. They lived in Cumberland Lodge in Windsor Great Park, close to Queen Victoria. The prince had come initially to England at the request of Queen Victoria in the

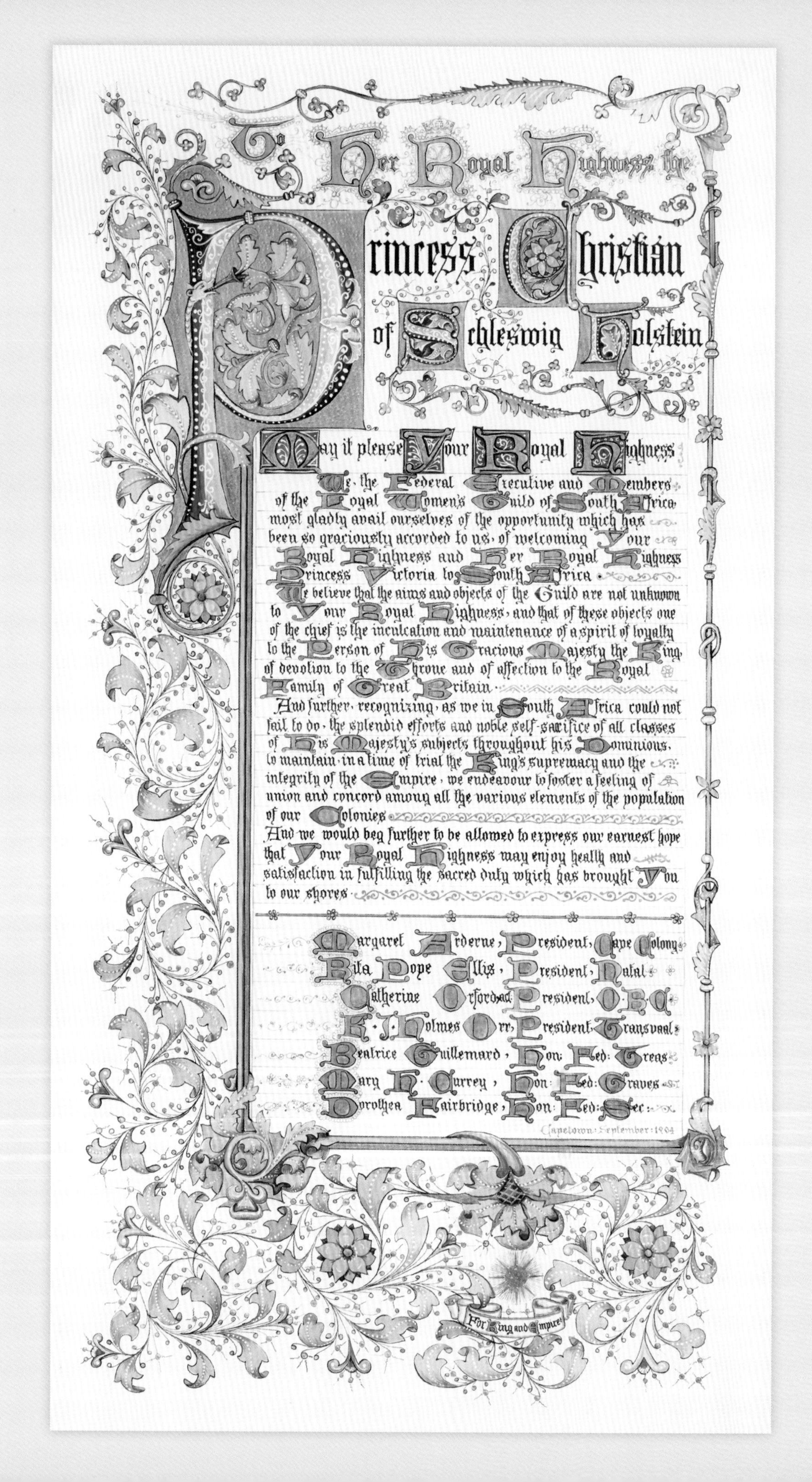

To Her Royal Highness the

Princess Christian of Schleswig Holstein

May it please Your Royal Highness

We, the Federal Executive and Members of the Loyal Women's Guild of South Africa most gladly avail ourselves of the opportunity which has been so graciously accorded to us, of welcoming Your Royal Highness and Her Royal Highness Princess Victoria to South Africa.

We believe that the aims and objects of the Guild are not unknown to Your Royal Highness, and that of these objects one of the chief is the inculcation and maintenance of a spirit of loyalty to the Person of His Gracious Majesty the King, of devotion to the Throne and of affection to the Royal Family of Great Britain.

And further, recognizing, as we in South Africa could not fail to do, the splendid efforts and noble self-sacrifice of all classes of His Majesty's subjects throughout his Dominions, to maintain in a time of trial the King's supremacy and the integrity of the Empire, we endeavour to foster a feeling of union and concord among all the various elements of the population of our Colonies

And we would beg further to be allowed to express our earnest hope that Your Royal Highness may enjoy health and satisfaction in fulfilling the sacred duty which has brought You to our shores.

Margaret Arderne, President, Cape Colony
Rita Pope Ellis, President, Natal
Catherine Orford, Ac: President, O.R.C.
K. J. Holmes Orr, President, Transvaal
Beatrice Guillemard, Hon: Fed: Treas:
Mary H. Currey, Hon: Fed: Graves
Dorothea Fairbridge, Hon: Fed: Sec:

Capetown: September: 1904

assumption that he was to be a potential new husband for her, rather than her daughter.

The marriage caused a rift in her family, as Schleswig and Holstein were fought over in the Schleswig Wars (in which Prussia and Austria defeated Denmark) and the Austro-Prussian War (in which Prussia defeated Austria). Alexandra, wife of the Prince of Wales and daughter of the King of Denmark (and also a third cousin to Prince Christian) supported Denmark's claim to Schleswig and Holstein. Princess Alice, Queen Victoria's second eldest daughter, also opposed the marriage. However, Queen Victoria and her eldest daughter Victoria, who was a personal friend of Prince Christian's family, supported the prince's claim and the marriage.

The couple had six children, although two did not live long, and led a relatively quiet and happy life. Princess Christian worked for her mother as a junior secretary. She suffered health problems and was addicted to opium and laudanum. She was very active in royal engagements and charities, being a founding member of the Red Cross. Prince Christian died in 1917 and she in 1923.

The address to Princess Christian of Schleswig-Holstein given in 1904, illuminated in Capetown.

Prince
The Prince of Teck

Each senior member of our present royal family undertakes a large number of engagements every year. Most are likely to be goodwill visits, perhaps to open a new building or to celebrate an anniversary. It is also likely that there will be a gift of some kind, given in thanks.

Past royalty also had this role and illuminated presentations were commonly used for gifts.

One example is a folder given to the Prince of Teck in 1870 for attending the festival to celebrate the fifty-fifth anniversary of the Royal Caledonian Asylum in Holloway.

In 1870 the asylum was situated on the Caledonian Road, London, a road that begins near King's Cross and heads north. The asylum had been founded earlier in the century, based in Islington. In the early 1900s it moved to Bushy, Hertfordshire, now the home of the Purcell School of Music.

For most of its existence, the asylum was a charity for the education and support of the children of Scottish servicemen and the orphans of Scottish Londoners. The proceeds of the sale to the Purcell School of Music were used to fund the Royal Caledonian Education Trust, to continue the charity's aims.

The Prince of Teck was Queen Mary's father, Queen Mary being the wife of King George V.

The Prince of Teck was born in Slavonia, now part of Croatia, as Francis, Duke of Teck, the son of Duke Alexander of Württemberg

ROYAL
CALEDONIAN
ASYLUM

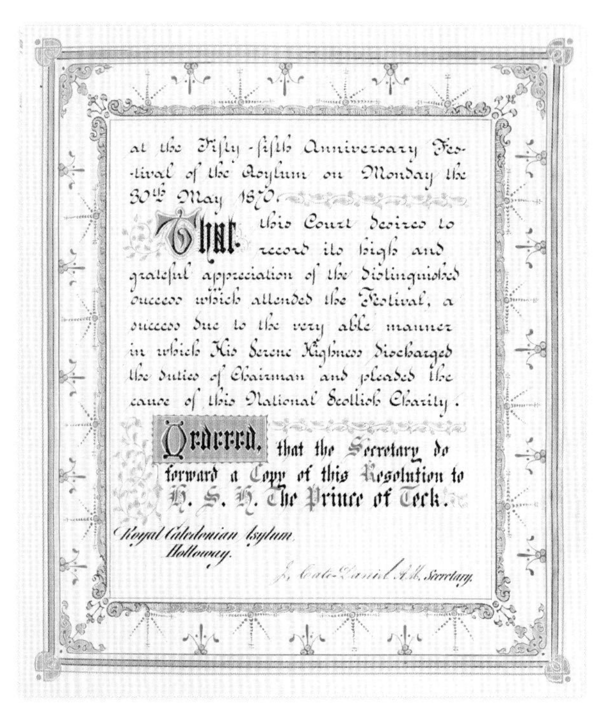

at the Fifty-fifth Anniversary Festival of the Asylum on Monday the 30th May 1870.

That this Court desires to record its high and grateful appreciation of the distinguished success which attended the Festival, a success due to the very able manner in which His Serene Highness discharged the duties of Chairman and pleaded the cause of this National Scottish Charity.

Ordered, that the Secretary do forward a Copy of this Resolution to H. S. H. The Prince of Teck.

Royal Caledonian Asylum,
Holloway.

J. Cato-Daniel A.M. Secretary.

The address to the Prince of Teck given in 1870.

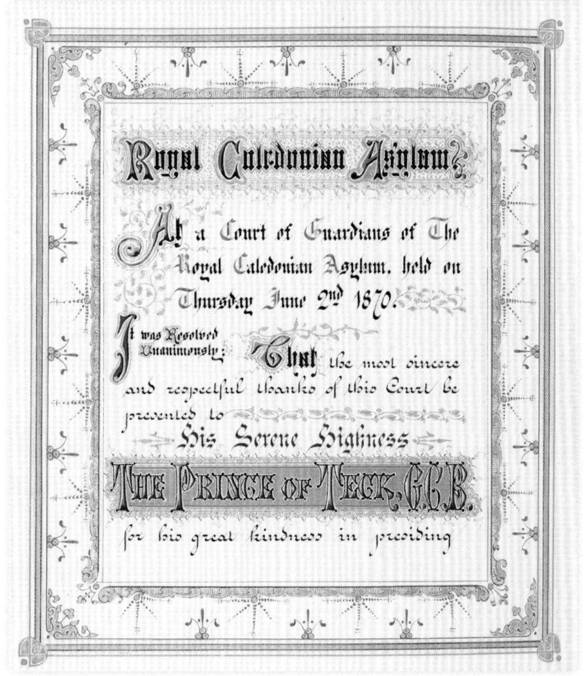

Royal Caledonian Asylum.

At a Court of Guardians of The Royal Caledonian Asylum, held on Thursday June 2nd 1870.

It was Resolved Unanimously: That the most sincere and respectful thanks of this Court be presented to

His Serene Highness

THE PRINCE OF TECK, G.C.B.

for his great kindness in presiding

and Countess Claudine von Rhédey von Kis-Rhéde. He became an officer in the Austrian army and was created the Prince of Teck in the Kingdom of Württemberg in 1863. He left the army when he married Princess Mary Adelaide of Cambridge in 1866, the younger daughter of Prince Adolphus, Duke of Cambridge, and a granddaughter of King George III and a cousin of Queen Victoria. They lived in Kensington Palace and White Lodge in Richmond Park. They had one daughter, Princess Victoria Mary Augusta Louise Olga Pauline Claudine Agnes of Teck, and three sons.

Princess Victoria Mary was initially engaged to Prince Albert Victor, Duke of Clarence, son of the Prince and Princess of Wales (later King Edward VII and his wife Queen Alexandra), but he died a few weeks later of the influenza pandemic. Instead, the princess married Prince Albert's brother, Prince George, Duke of York. Therefore, she became Queen Mary and Empress of India. She died in 1953 at the beginning of the reign of her granddaughter, Queen Elizabeth II.

The Prince of Teck died in 1900 at White Lodge.

Visit by a princess
Princess Alice, Countess of Athlone

Princess Alice was born in Windsor Castle in 1883. She was named Alice Mary Victoria Augusta Pauline, with the title Her Royal Highness Princess Alice of Albany. She also received the titles Princess of Saxe-Coburg and Gotha, and the Duchess of Saxony. She was born to Prince Leopold, Duke of Albany (the youngest son of Queen Victoria) and Princess Helena of Waldeck and Pyrmont. Queen Victoria was one of her godmothers.

Princess Alice had a younger brother, Prince Charles Edward, but unfortunately Prince Leopold died before his son's birth. Prince Charles Edward studied in Bonn and became close to Kaiser Wilhelm II. When the First World War began, he became a general in the German army and his British titles were removed in 1919. He later joined the Nazi Party and his three sons fought for Germany in the Second World War. He was imprisoned after the war and his sister, Princess Alice, visited Germany to plead, unsuccessfully, for his release.

Princess Alice was married at Windsor in 1904 to Prince Alexander of Teck, the brother of Princess Mary, the Princess of Wales, who married King George V and became Queen Mary. On her marriage, Princess Alice became HRH Princess Alexander of Teck. She had three children but one died in infancy. She was a haemophilia gene carrier, inherited from her father.

In 1917 all Germanic titles were changed, and Prince Alexander of Teck took the surname Cambridge and became, briefly, Lord Cambridge and then the Earl of Athlone. In 1924 he was appointed the Governor General of South Africa, with Princess Alice becoming the vicereine. Lord Athlone and Princess Alice returned to England in 1931.

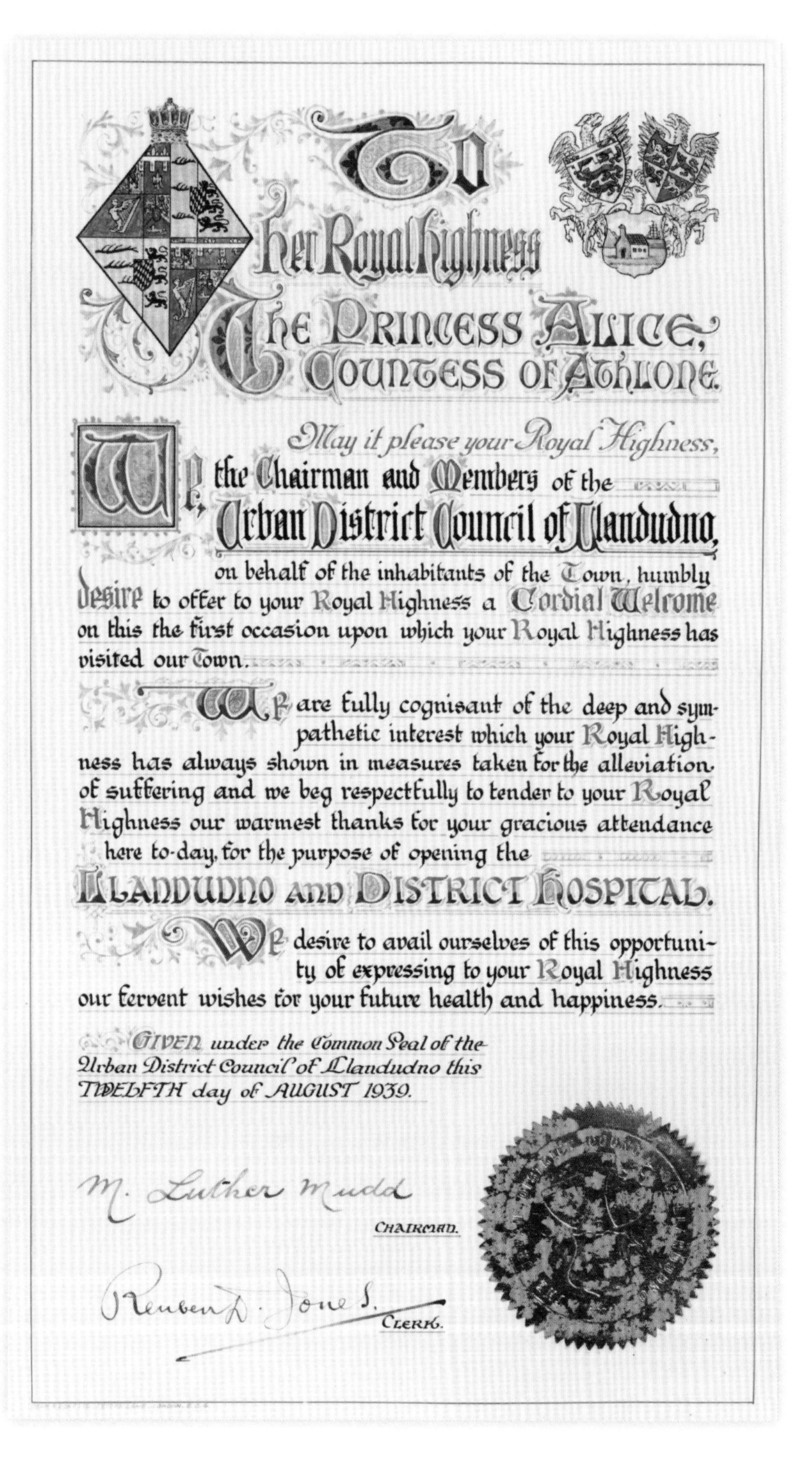

To Her Royal Highness The Princess Alice, Countess of Athlone.

May it please your Royal Highness,

We, the Chairman and Members of the Urban District Council of Llandudno, on behalf of the inhabitants of the Town, humbly desire to offer to your Royal Highness a Cordial Welcome on this the first occasion upon which your Royal Highness has visited our Town.

We are fully cognisant of the deep and sympathetic interest which your Royal Highness has always shown in measures taken for the alleviation of suffering and we beg respectfully to tender to your Royal Highness our warmest thanks for your gracious attendance here to-day, for the purpose of opening the Llandudno and District Hospital.

We desire to avail ourselves of this opportunity of expressing to your Royal Highness our fervent wishes for your future health and happiness.

Given under the Common Seal of the Urban District Council of Llandudno this Twelfth day of August 1939.

M. Luther Mudd
Chairman.

Reuben D. Jones.
Clerk.

In 1939 Princess Alice visited Llandudno to open a hospital and was presented with a pretty illuminated scroll by the Chairman and Urban District Council of Llandudno.

Lord Athlone became Governor General of Canada from 1940–46, with Princess Alice becoming a vicereine once again. When in England, Lord Athlone and Princess Alice lived at Kensington Palace, where Lord Athlone died in 1957. Princess Alice died in 1981 at the age of ninety-seven, the last grandchild of Queen Victoria and the longest-lived British princess by descent.

The address to Princess Alice, Countess of Athlone given in 1939, illuminated by Shaw & Sons, Fetter Lane, London

SPORT

Footballer
James W. Lewis

Football has significantly changed over the years. The top professional players are very well paid and the teams have many international players and managers. What a different situation to that in place only a few years ago!

James (Jim) Lewis Sr was a footballer from a different age, a time when there were many amateurs who played the sport in addition to their normal day jobs. Jim was a toy shop owner as well as a keen amateur footballer playing for Walthamstow Avenue, one of the best amateur teams in the country. He also played for his country, participated in 120 matches and was recognised for his great contribution by the Football Association in 1942 with a stylish illuminated presentation.

James Lewis as a boy.

Jim had two sons: the older was also named Jim, who also joined Walthamstow aged sixteen in 1943. Jim Sr and Jim Jr played together until the latter was sent on National Service to India. On his return, he re-joined Walthamstow which won the FA Amateur Cup in 1952 at Wembley in front of 100,000 people. In the next season Walthamstow went out in the fourth round of the FA Cup, playing Manchester United, Jim Jr having scored three goals. He was signed by the Chelsea Manager, Ted Drake, in late 1952. Jim Jr refused to turn professional. He worked as a travelling salesman for Thermos flasks and earned more as a salesman – £20 a week – than he could earn as a footballer, and he got a car. Few footballers could afford such a luxury. His employer was generous with time off to train and play. Chelsea won the First Division league title in 1954–5. He also played for Great Britain in the 1952 (Helsinki), 1956 (Melbourne) and 1960 (Rome) Olympics.

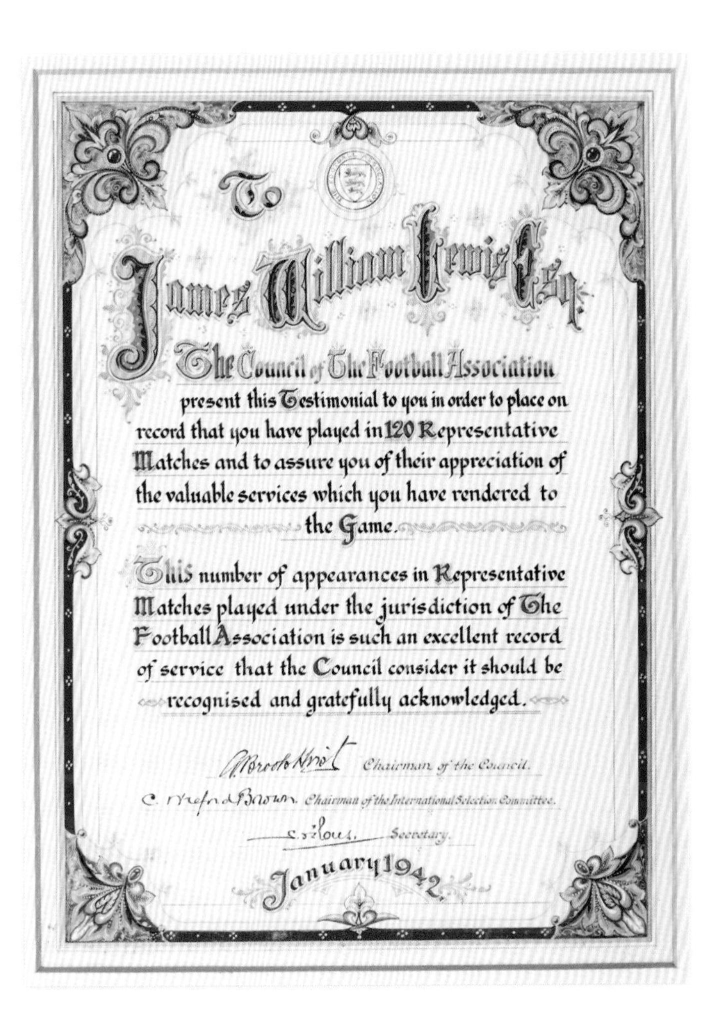

To

James William Lewis Esq.

The Council of The Football Association

present this Testimonial to you in order to place on record that you have played in 120 Representative Matches and to assure you of their appreciation of the valuable services which you have rendered to the Game.

This number of appearances in Representative Matches played under the jurisdiction of The Football Association is such an excellent record of service that the Council consider it should be recognised and gratefully acknowledged.

Chairman of the Council.

Chairman of the International Selection Committee.

Secretary.

January 1942.

The address to James Lewis given in 1942.

Amateur status was removed by the Football Association in 1974 because of the frequency of secret payments to amateurs. In 2005 Jim Jr was invited back to Chelsea when the team won the Premier title, fifty years after its first success.

Walthamstow Avenue Football Club ceased to exist in 1988 when it merged with Leytonstone, which then became Redbridge Forest, and subsequently Dagenham and Redbridge.

Football club
Oxford City Football Club

The manner in which football leagues are organised, especially those below the top four divisions (the Football League), can be confusing. Below this is the National League, which is comprised of seven groups or steps. The rest is too complicated to describe here!

Oxford City Football Club was formed in 1882. The club reached the finals of the Amateur Cup Competition three times between 1902 and 1913, winning the cup once in 1906 and being runners-up twice. It joined the Isthmian League in 1907. The club had eight players who gained international caps. Despite its early success, the club declined over the twentieth century. The Football Association Council gave Oxford City Football Club a colourful, charming illuminated certificate in 1958 in celebration of its anniversary of existence for seventy-five years.

In 1979 there was an effort to reverse the decline of the club when it became a limited company. Bobby Moore became its manager with Harry Redknapp his assistant manager. In 1988 the club lost its grounds and it was forced to resign from the Isthmian League. In 1990 it joined the South Midlands League Division One and won promotion, returning to the Isthmian League in 1993 and moving to its current ground in Marsh Lane Marston, near Oxford.

Oxford City is not to be confused with the more successful Oxford United, which began as Headington United in 1893, changed its name in 1960, entered the Football League in 1962 and won the League Cup in 1986.

The address to Oxford City Football Club in 1958, illuminated by C.W. Harris, 28 King Street, London.

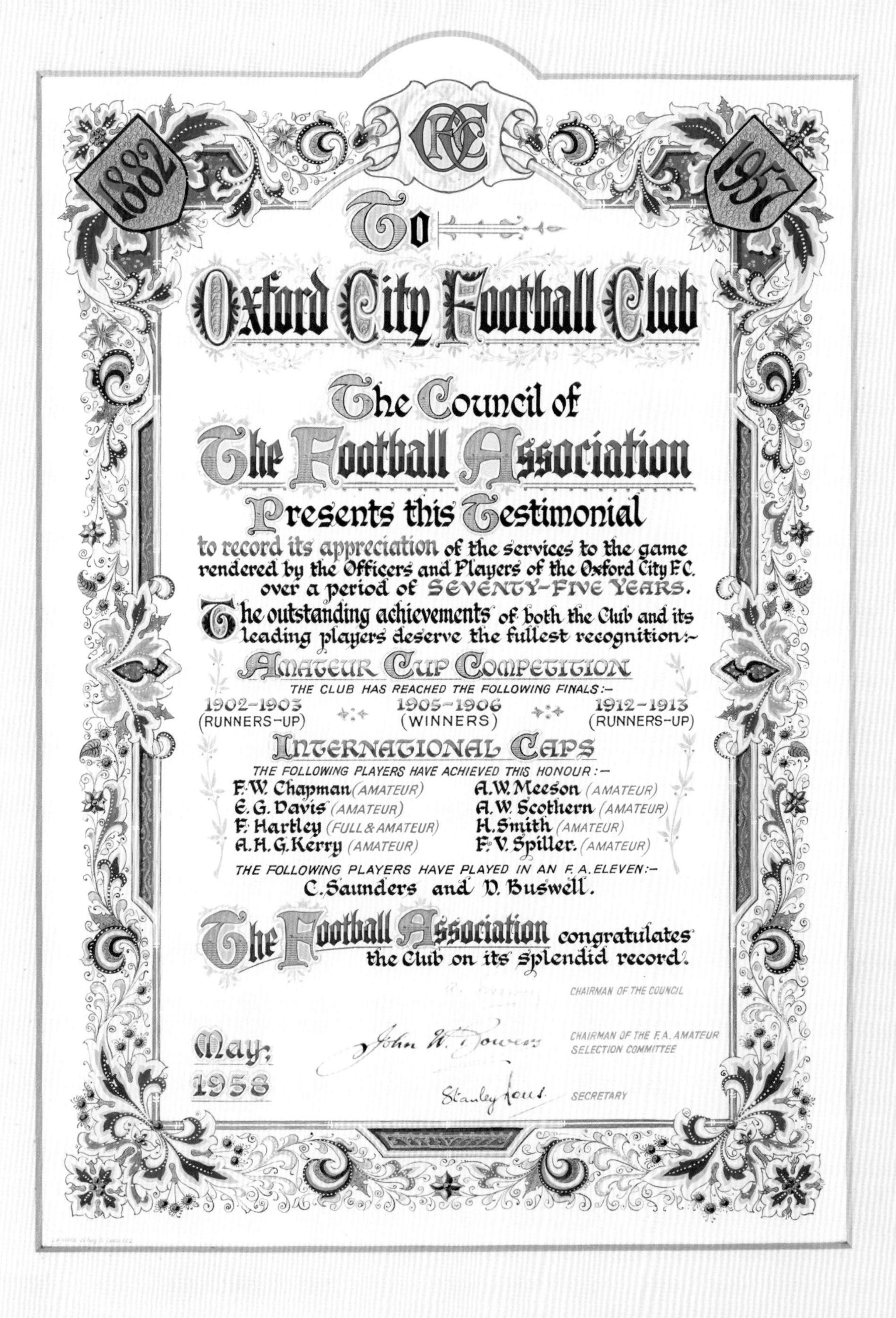

1882

1957

OCFC

To

Oxford City Football Club

The Council of

The Football Association

Presents this Testimonial

to record its appreciation of the services to the game rendered by the Officers and Players of the Oxford City F.C. over a period of SEVENTY-FIVE YEARS.

The outstanding achievements of both the Club and its leading players deserve the fullest recognition:-

AMATEUR CUP COMPETITION

THE CLUB HAS REACHED THE FOLLOWING FINALS:-

1902-1903 (RUNNERS-UP)

1905-1906 (WINNERS)

1912-1913 (RUNNERS-UP)

INTERNATIONAL CAPS

THE FOLLOWING PLAYERS HAVE ACHIEVED THIS HONOUR:-

F. W. Chapman (AMATEUR)

E. G. Davis (AMATEUR)

F. Hartley (FULL & AMATEUR)

A. H. G. Kerry (AMATEUR)

A. W. Meeson (AMATEUR)

A. W. Scothern (AMATEUR)

H. Smith (AMATEUR)

F. V. Spiller. (AMATEUR)

THE FOLLOWING PLAYERS HAVE PLAYED IN AN F.A. ELEVEN:-

C. Saunders and D. Buswell.

The Football Association congratulates the Club on its splendid record.

CHAIRMAN OF THE COUNCIL

May, 1958

CHAIRMAN OF THE F.A. AMATEUR SELECTION COMMITTEE

SECRETARY

STAFF SERVICE

Shop worker
Mr C.R. Pitt

This is an unusual illuminated address as it is addressed to C.R.P. in 1939, but has no other indication of who this may be. However, it arrived with another address dated 1938 to Mr C.R. Pitt. We are not told what names C.R. stand for.

Both presentations were from his employers, Debenham & Freebody. The first was to celebrate forty years of work since 1898, and the second was for his retirement the following year. Unfortunately, we do not know what role he had at the store.

There are twenty-four pages in a small folder, each with a pretty flower garland at each corner. Every page records the names of the staff of Debenham & Freebody in each of their departments, in alphabetic order. The capital initial of the department name is embellished, copying the practice of historic books of hours which often enlarged and highlighted the first letter of new sections of text. The departments include many that would not be readily recognised today such as Corsets, Fancy, Mantles and Tea Gowns.

In 1939, Debenham and Freebody was in a grand building at 27–37 Wigmore Street, London, a shopping street parallel and close to Oxford Street. The shop started as a drapers store in the eighteenth century. William Debenham joined the drapers and the shop name became Clark & Debenham. The business expanded and became Debenham, Son & Freebody in the mid-1800s, with shops in London, Cheltenham and Harrogate. The name Debenhams Limited was created in the early 1900s, but shops still retained their earlier names.

The address to C.R. Pitt given in 1939.

DEBENHAM AND FREEBODY

1898 — 1939

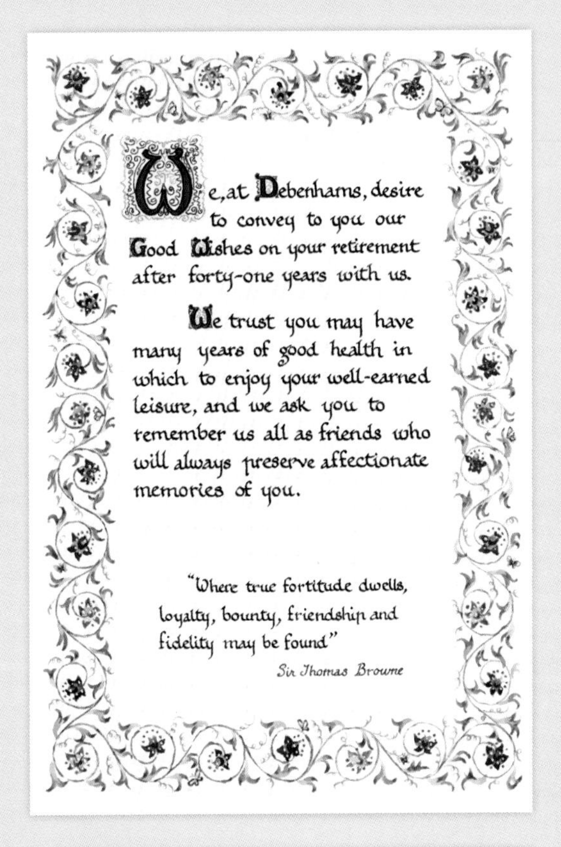

We, at Debenhams, desire to convey to you our Good Wishes on your retirement after forty-one years with us.

We trust you may have many years of good health in which to enjoy your well-earned leisure, and we ask you to remember us all as friends who will always preserve affectionate memories of you.

"Where true fortitude dwells, loyalty, bounty, friendship and fidelity may be found"

Sir Thomas Browne

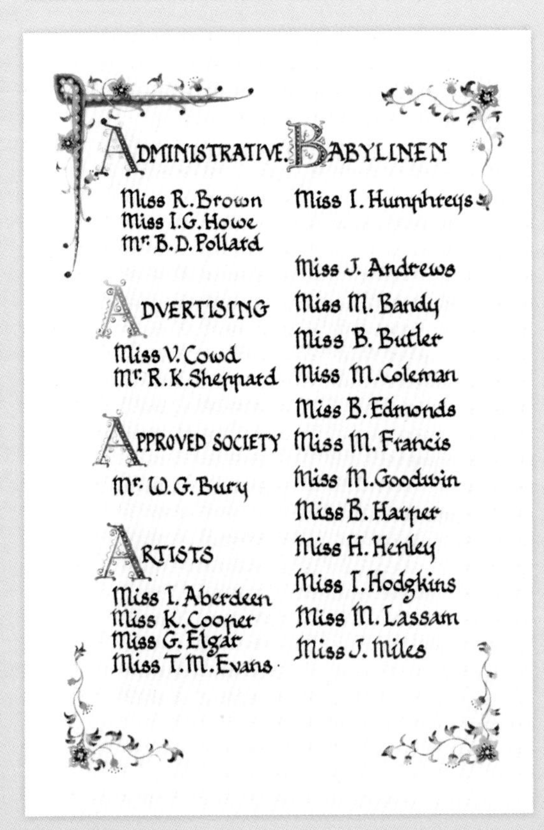

ADMINISTRATIVE

Miss R. Brown
Miss I.G. Howe
Mr. B.D. Pollard

ADVERTISING

Miss V. Cowd
Mr. R.K. Sheppard

APPROVED SOCIETY

Mr. W.G. Bury

ARTISTS

Miss I. Aberdeen
Miss K. Cooper
Miss G. Elgar
Miss T.M. Evans

BABYLINEN

Miss I. Humphreys

Miss J. Andrews
Miss M. Bandy
Miss B. Butler
Miss M. Coleman
Miss B. Edmonds
Miss M. Francis
Miss M. Goodwin
Miss B. Harper
Miss H. Henley
Miss I. Hodgkins
Miss M. Lassam
Miss J. Miles

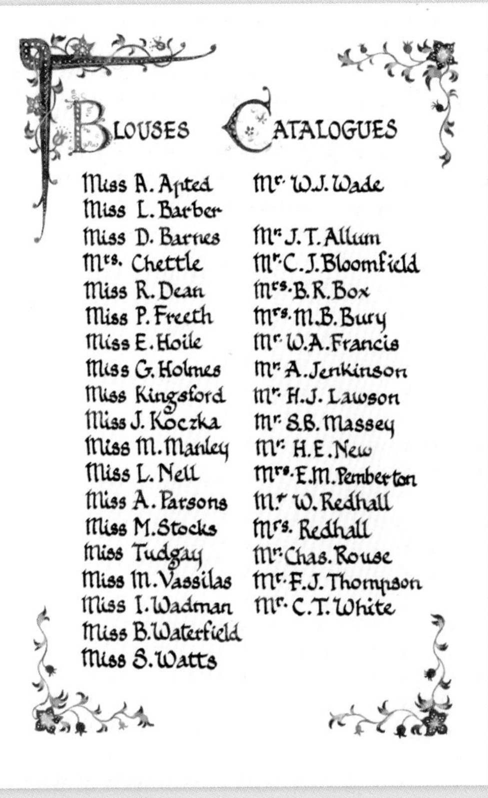

BLOUSES

Miss A. Apted
Miss L. Barber
Miss D. Barnes
Mrs. Chettle
Miss R. Dean
Miss P. Freeth
Miss E. Hoile
Miss G. Holmes
Miss Kingsford
Miss J. Koczka
Miss M. Manley
Miss L. Nell
Miss A. Parsons
Miss M. Stocks
Miss Tudgay
Miss M. Vassilas
Miss I. Wadman
Miss B. Waterfield
Miss S. Watts

CATALOGUES

Mr. W.J. Wade

Mr. J.T. Allum
Mr. C.J. Bloomfield
Mrs. B.R. Box
Mrs. M.B. Bury
Mr. W.A. Francis
Mr. A. Jenkinson
Mr. H.J. Lawson
Mr. S.B. Massey
Mr. H.E. New
Mrs. E.M. Pemberton
Mr. W. Redhall
Mrs. Redhall
Mr. Chas. Rouse
Mr. F.J. Thompson
Mr. C.T. White

Railwayman
David Morgan

David Morgan was the Traffic Manager of the Rhondda Branches of the Taff Valley Railway in Glamorgan. He resigned in 1883 after thirty-six years of service and was given an unusual illumination with a beautiful blue edging.

The Taff Valley Railway was one of the oldest railways in Wales, operating from 1836 until 1922 when it became part of the Great Western Railway, and from 1948 part of British Railways. The railway was needed to transport coal and iron from the South Wales valleys ready for shipping.

George Stephenson built the first public railway line in the world to use steam locomotives in 1830. Robert Stephenson, George's son, designed Stephenson's Rocket in 1829, which was the most advanced locomotive of its time for the Liverpool and Manchester Railway and the basis for design of steam engines for the next 150 years.

However, it was Richard Trevithick who first built a high-pressure steam engine and the first working railway steam locomotive in 1804 for use in Merthyr Tydfil. The world's first steam train travelled from Merthyr Tydfil ironworks for 9 miles. However, this was short-lived, as the tracks were not strong enough for the heavy engine. Isambard Kingdom Brunel was asked to calculate the cost of a railway from Merthyr Tydfil to Cardiff in 1835 (£190,000) and a company, the Taff Vale Railway, was created in 1836. A Rhondda branch line was opened in 1841. At its height, the busiest station on the Taff Vale Railway, Pontypridd, with its one-third of a mile long platform, had two trains a minute passing. The trains carried both minerals and passengers.

The address to David Morgan given in 1883.

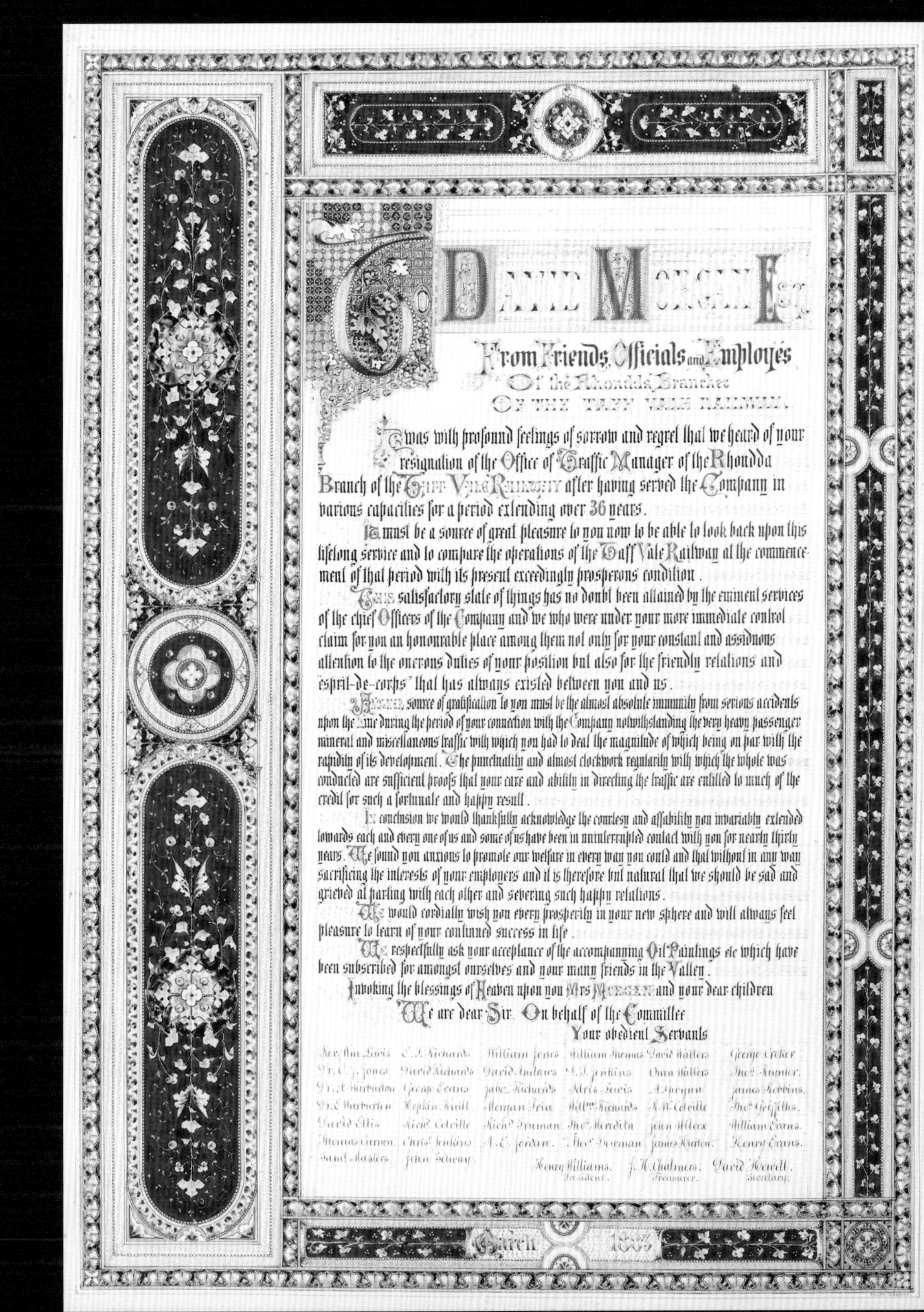
To David Morgan Esq.

From Friends, Officials and Employés
Of the Rhondda Branches
Of the Taff Vale Railway.

It was with profound feelings of sorrow and regret that we heard of your resignation of the Office of Traffic Manager of the Rhondda Branch of the Taff Vale Railway after having served the Company in various capacities for a period extending over 36 years.

It must be a source of great pleasure to you now to be able to look back upon this lifelong service and to compare the operations of the Taff Vale Railway at the commencement of that period with its present exceedingly prosperous condition.

This satisfactory state of things has no doubt been attained by the eminent services of the chief Officers of the Company and we who were under your more immediate control claim for you an honourable place among them not only for your constant and assiduous attention to the onerous duties of your position but also for the friendly relations and "esprit-de-corps" that has always existed between you and us.

Another source of gratification to you must be the almost absolute immunity from serious accidents upon the Line during the period of your connection with the Company notwithstanding the very heavy passenger mineral and miscellaneous traffic with which you had to deal the magnitude of which being on par with the rapidity of its development. The punctuality and almost clockwork regularity with which the whole was conducted are sufficient proofs that your care and ability in directing the traffic are entitled to much of the credit for such a fortunate and happy result.

In conclusion we would thankfully acknowledge the courtesy and affability you invariably extended towards each and every one of us and some of us have been in uninterrupted contact with you for nearly thirty years. We found you anxious to promote our welfare in every way you could and that without in any way sacrificing the interests of your employers and it is therefore but natural that we should be sad and grieved at parting with each other and severing such happy relations.

We would cordially wish you every prosperity in your new sphere and will always feel pleasure to learn of your continued success in life.

We respectfully ask your acceptance of the accompanying Oil Paintings etc which have been subscribed for amongst ourselves and your many friends in the Valley.

Invoking the blessings of Heaven upon you Mrs Morgan and your dear children

We are dear Sir. On behalf of the Committee

Your obedient Servants

Rev. Wm Lewis, Dr. C. J. Jones, Dr. A. Warburton, Dr. E. Warburton, David Ellis, Thomas Curnow, Saml. Masters, E. J. Richards, David Richards, George Evans, Hopkin Knill, Richd. Colville, Chrisr. Jenkins, John Selway, William Jones, David Andrews, Jabez Richards, Morgan Price, Richd. Truman, A. E. Jordan, William Thomas, D. J. Jenkins, Idris Lewis, Willm. Richards, Thos. Meredith, Alexr. Bowman, David Walters, Owen Walters, A. Gwynn, R. W. Colville, John Wilcox, James Hurton, George Crocker, Thos. Turner, James Robbins, Thos. Griffiths, William Evans, Henry Evans.

Henry Williams. President.
J. H. Chalmers. Treasurer.
David Howell. Secretary.

March 1883

Water manager
William Terrey

In 1930, William Terrey was thanked by the Water Committee of Sheffield for his services as General Manager of the Water Undertaking by being presented with a fine illuminated address on his retirement.

Terrey had studied engineering at the University of Nottingham before joining the Nottingham Water Company as Chief Assistant to Henry Role MICE (Member of the Institution of Civil Engineers). He moved to Sheffield in 1888 when the Sheffield Water Works transferred from the company to the corporation. Sheffield was the first corporation to use compulsory purchase powers to take over its water supply. The corporation paid £2m.

William Terrey.

Terrey was involved with a number of significant improvements to Sheffield's water supply. For instance, he was the principal witness in the promotion of a Bill for the acquisition of the waters of the Little Don Valley. He redesigned the reservoirs and pumping station and was recognised for saving the corporation a substantial £240,000. The Little Don rises in the Peak District and flows down into the River Don.

Terrey wrote about his work in *The Sheffield Water Supply*, published in 1929.

The address to William Terrey given in 1930, illuminated by C.W. Norris, 34 King Street, Cheapside, London.

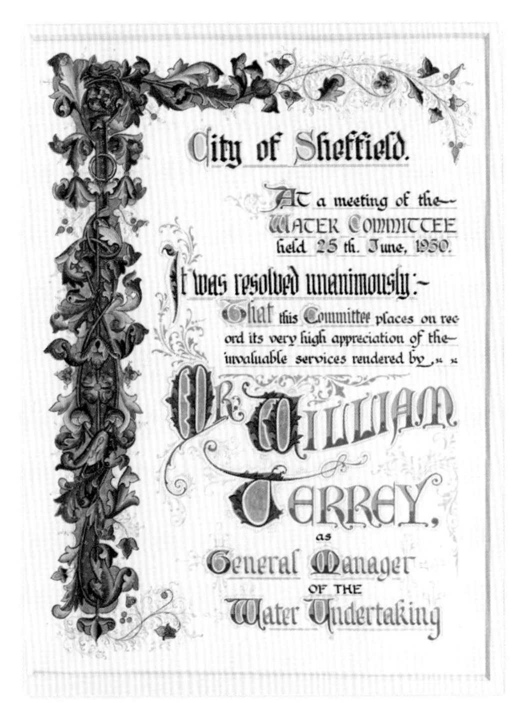

City of Sheffield.

At a meeting of the Water Committee held 25 th. June, 1950.

It was resolved unanimously:-

That this Committee places on record its very high appreciation of the invaluable services rendered by

Mr. William Terrey,

as

General Manager of the Water Undertaking

Since the transfer to the Corporation of the undertaking in 1888. He has served the City with unswerving faithfulness and assiduous devotion, which has very largely contributed to the enormous development and success of the undertaking.

That a copy of this resolution, under the Corporate Common Seal, be presented to Mr. Terrey.

The foregoing resolution was confirmed by the City Council on the 2nd. July, 1950.

Lord Mayor.

William E. Hart Town Clerk

BANK OF ENGLAND

The directors

This is a simple illuminated address, given to the directors of the Bank of England at the end of 1945. It is in gratitude from the City of London to the Bank of England for storing archives and treasures during the Second World War.

The illuminated address has a nice signature of the City of London Town Clerk, Alfred Thomas Roach, based at the Guildhall. It also names 'Davis Mayor', Sir Charles Davis, who had been elected Lord Mayor of London in 1945.

The Bank of England was a good place for storing and protecting the City of London's archives. It has three floors below ground level and the gold remained in the sub-vault throughout the war years. The building was never hit by a bomb, but did receive minor damage when the road outside was hit.

The archives held by the Bank of England are readily accessed by viewing the online catalogue of archive records at www.bankofengland.co.uk/archive. It is also possible to visit the Bank of England and view the original documents.

The address to the directors of the Bank of England given in 1945, with the kind permission of the Bank of England Archivist, reference number (13A84/7/50).

Davis Mayor

A Common Council holden in the Guildhall of the City of London on Thursday the 29th day of November, 1945.

Resolved Unanimously :–

That the thanks of this Court be accorded to the Directors of the Bank of England for much valued accommodation generously afforded for the safe storage of this Corporation's archives, books and antiquities during the period of hostilities.

That the thanks of this Court be also accorded to the Officers of the Bank for their constant care and help.

Roach

First published by Unicorn
an imprint of Unicorn Publishing Group LLP, 2021
5 Newburgh Street
London W1F 7RG
www.unicornpublishing.org

Text © John P. Wilson

10 9 8 7 6 5 4 3 2 1

ISBN 978-1-913491-37-6

Designed by Matthew Wilson / mexington.co.uk

Printed in the EU

All rights reserved. No part of the contents of this book may be reproduced, stored in or introduced into a retrieval system, or transmitted, in any form or by any means (electronic, mechanical, photocopying, recording or otherwise), without the prior written permission of the copyright holder and the above publisher of this book.

Every effort has been made to trace copyright holders and to obtain their permission for the use of copyright material. The publisher apologises for any errors or omissions contained within and would be grateful if notified of any corrections that should be incorporated in future reprints or editions of this book.